i wish
i was
worse

i wish
i was
worse

shirin delalat

i wish i was worse

First Edition
Published by sdinsd, San Diego, CA

This is a work of memoir. Events and conversations are recreated from memory. Some names, identifying characteristics, and chronologies have been changed to protect the privacy of those depicted. Any resemblance to persons whom I actively dislike, however, is probably intentional.

Library of Congress Control Number: 2025906102
ISBN: 979-8-9918815-5-5

Printed in the United States of America

The author acknowledges that this book was written by a gloriously difficult human, equal parts wildfire and precision, who says shit that makes people squirm, feels everything at full volume, and won't water herself down to quench your thirst for proper. Not acknowledging that would be "worse," but in that pathetic, self-erasing way that transforms women into well-behaved ghosts. The kind of "worse" I'm championing tells the truth even when it ruins the vibe and gets you uninvited from boring dinner parties. If you came here for inspirational quotes to cross-stitch on throw pillows, you've made a terrible purchase. If your idea of a good time is raw truths delivered with unflinching honesty, you're exactly the kind of worse I wrote this for. This book pairs well with a blunt object and the urge to say something you can't take back. Consider yourself warned. Or welcomed. Your choice.

Blog: www.sdinsd.com
Book: www.iwishiwasworse.com

for g,
the heartbeat behind every page.
someday, i'll be gone, but these words will remain.
in them, find the truth i've always known:
you were the greatest gift i was ever given.

for kb,
thanks for loving me,
even when all i did was thank you for it.
p.s. you really did give me the world.

for david sedaris,
who told me this would make a better first line than title.
i have a long and proud history of ignoring men's advice.

contents

disclaimer:
i mean every word

The polite thing would be to ease you in gently. Tell you this gets dark but there's light at the end.

I'm not interested in being polite. And there's no light. Just different kinds of fire.

I didn't write this to make peace. I wrote it as creative justice. Because the vindictive goblin that lives in my soul made me.

Spite is a terrible reason to write a book.
And yet, nothing motivates me more.

This isn't a story about healing. It's a story about remembering. About the versions of myself I exiled.

The loud one. The selfish one. The angry one.

I unleashed them.

They came back louder. Meaner. Ready to burn it all down.

I didn't write this to be palatable or poetic. I wrote it the way you scream into a pillow when no one's listening. I wrote it for the girl who stayed quiet long enough for a villain origin story to marinate, and for the woman who finally stopped caring who was comfortable.

Sometimes I'm an unreliable narrator just because it's more fun that way.

Every time I sit down to write, it feels like I'm dismantling a bomb.
One wrong move, and everything explodes.
But the right one?
That's when the real damage begins.
That's when it gets interesting.

You won't agree with everything. Good. That means it's honest.

This book isn't neat. It's not wrapped in a bow or softened with euphemisms. It has bite marks, side-eyes, and stories that should've stayed secrets. It's rage and tenderness tangled together. Because that's how life actually feels.

You're going to put this book down at least twice. Once because I said something you weren't ready to hear. Once because you recognized yourself and didn't like the view.

The question is whether you'll pick it back up.

No apologies. No redemptions. No moral of the story.

Just me, saying the things I was never supposed to say.
Out loud. In print. Knowing how deep it might cut.

If you picked this up because you know me and you're
hoping not to see yourself in these pages...
You should've behaved better.

I'm petty and quick-witted.
That's a dangerous combination.

This might ruin your day.
Frankly, I hope it does.

I mean every word.

I'm not clearing any rumors.
I probably did it.
And something worse.

the myth of the "good" girl

I was never the good girl.

Not the quiet one who swallowed her words like bitter medicine. Not the agreeable one who nodded until her neck ached. Not the one who made herself smaller and smaller until she practically vanished.

The world wanted me to sand down my edges. To speak in whispers. To apologize for existing too loudly.

But I was born with fangs.

This book isn't about finding myself. It's about burning down the prison of expectations and dancing in the ashes. There's no redemption arc here. No moment where I learn to be sweeter, smaller, more digestible.

I didn't become better.

I became worse.

Worse at shrinking myself to fit into rooms I never wanted to be in.
Worse at saying thank you for crumbs I was never actually hungry for.
Worse at twisting myself into the version of me that made other people feel comfortable.
And worst of all?
I stopped caring how the world saw me.

And in that beautiful, deliberate failure…I found something the people invested in my silence never wanted me to discover.

Freedom.

The kind that makes other people nervous.
The kind that's contagious.

Because being the "good" girl: it's just another word for disappearing while standing right in front of them.

I don't wish I was better.

I wish I was worse.

...

There are facts.
And there's what's true.
I'm not here to untangle them.
I'm here to hold both and write anyway.

...

Don't mistake this for another guide to becoming better.

This isn't advice. It's a dare.
A dare to become worse: louder, messier, feral, diabolical.

Being "good" is just compliance in a cute outfit. The path to freedom is through being shamelessly, strategically bad at everything that diminishes you.

I learned this the hard way.
I learned it when I miscarried and smiled for photos at a wedding the next day. Being "fine" was easier than admitting I wasn't.

Through all the moments when being "good" cost me pieces of my soul and being "worse" saved what remained.

I learned it when the same people who kept breaking me praised me for being resilient.
I learned it when I walked away from a job that valued my output over my humanity.
I learned it when I stopped explaining myself to people who were committed to misunderstanding me.
When I refused to stop breastfeeding my toddler because it made someone uncomfortable.
When I disappointed people who expected my compliance and burned bridges that only led to places I didn't want to go.

This is that story. My story.
But maybe it's yours too.

Maybe you're tired of dulling your blade to spare the ones who keep testing its edge.

Maybe you're ready to embrace being worse.
More fun at parties.

You might lose people.

You'll get yourself back.

...

It starts early.

I watched it happen to other girls first. The praise for sitting still. For sharing their toys when they didn't want to. For swallowing their words when they disagreed.

"Good girl," they'd say, and something in those girls would light up. Hungry for that approval. Desperate to earn it again.

I learned the rules by watching. Being good meant being loved. Being difficult meant being left behind.

I knew what was expected of me.
The world wanted me to soften myself.
Smooth down the sharp edges that made people flinch.
Stay quiet when every cell in my body was screaming to speak.
Say yes when no was sitting on my tongue like poison I was afraid to spit out.

Being good was supposed to be the goal. Not happy. Not honest. Not whole.

Just good.

That's how it's supposed to work, anyway. But I didn't play by those rules. I wasn't the dutiful daughter who listened quietly and followed orders. I was raised in a culture where respect and obedience were paramount, but even as a child, I pushed back.

Being Iranian-American meant the contradictions came early.

One culture prized quiet compliance, especially for girls.

The other preached individualism, but still preferred its women agreeable.

I couldn't settle for either version.

Not to be rebellious for the sake of it, but because I couldn't accept a version of myself that wasn't mine.

I wasn't polite when I didn't believe in what I was being asked to agree to. I wasn't quiet when I had something to say. I wasn't agreeable when something didn't sit right with me.

But that didn't mean the expectations weren't there.

They loomed over every girl, whether she leaned into them or not. I watched girls in school try to make themselves smaller, to be softer, to take up less space, because the alternative was being called unlikable. And for so many, unlikable was the ultimate failure.

I wasn't always likable. I never cared much about being likable.

Worse suited me better.

...

Second grade was when I found out I wasn't a "good girl."

Mrs. Peterson had us sitting in a circle for story time, all of us cross-legged on that scratchy carpet that smelled like disinfectant and broken dreams. She was reading something forgettable, one of those sterilized tales with a moral about sharing or kindness or some other virtue they were determined to drill into us until we bled compliance. The kind of story that makes you wonder who decided children needed to learn that self-preservation was selfish.

I raised my hand.

"But that doesn't make sense," I said when she called on me. "Why would the rabbit give away his carrot? He'd be hungry."

The other kids giggled. Not because I was wrong, because I said what they weren't brave enough to. That kind of laugh sticks with you.

Mrs. Peterson's lips thinned into that familiar line, the international symbol for "a child has just committed the crime of logic."

"Because sharing is caring, Shirin," she said, in that sticky sweet voice adults use when they're trying not to show their annoyance. "The rabbit cares more about his friends than about himself."

I remember thinking: *That's stupid. The rabbit should care about himself too.*

I said it out loud.
(That's where my villain arc began.)

The classroom went silent. Mrs. Peterson closed the book with a snap that felt like judgment.

"We'll discuss this after class," she said.

And we did. She told me I was being disruptive. That good students don't challenge their teachers. That good *girls* listen quietly.

It was my first lesson in the unwritten rulebook, the one handed down to girls from the moment they're born: Be small. Be sweet. Be selfless.

Be *good*.

I went home and told my dad what happened. I expected...I don't know. Not trouble, exactly. But some gentle correction, maybe. Some reminder about respecting my elders.

Instead, he laughed. A full, deep belly laugh that filled our kitchen.

"You're going to give them hell, aren't you?" he said, pride warming his voice. "Good."

That was my dad. The one person who never expected me to be anything but exactly what I was. When everyone else was trying to sand my edges smooth, he was admiring my angles.

God, I miss him.

...

I remember being in school and watching boys get away with everything. They'd talk back to teachers, push boundaries, and somehow still be labeled "boys being boys." The girls, though? We were expected to sit quietly, behave, and follow the rules. And if we didn't? We weren't just bad. We were *difficult*.

Fourth grade. Science class. We were building simple machines, and I wanted to design a better pulley than the one in our textbook. Mr. Hall told me to stick to the instructions.

"But this would work better," I insisted.

"Shirin," he sighed, "just follow directions like everyone else."

Two tables over, Brandon had completely abandoned the assignment to build some contraption of his own design. Mr. Hall walked by, chuckled, and said, "Quite the engineer, aren't you, buddy?"

The different standards were so glaringly obvious that even at eight years old, I recognized the hypocrisy. The casual acceptance that boys could color outside the lines, but girls needed to stay within them.

It stung.

...

High school was worse.

The rules got more complex, more suffocating. It wasn't just about being polite anymore. It was about being pretty, but not too pretty. Smart, but not too smart.

Ambitious, but not so ambitious that you intimidated the boys.

God forbid you intimidate the boys.

I was five foot one with opinions that didn't know how to stay quiet (they still don't). No one ever knew what to do with me. There's a fine line between what's acceptable and what's true. I don't tiptoe across it...I stomp.

"You'll never get a boyfriend that way," my mom warned, worry creasing her forehead.

As if that was the goal. As if the pinnacle of my existence was making myself small enough for a boy to feel comfortable picking me up.

That's the thing about refusing to play by the rules. It weeds people out.

The ones who need you to be good, to be agreeable, to be less than you are...they fall away.

What remains are the people who love you not despite your fire, but because of it.

My dad. My brother, in his way. A handful of friends who didn't run when I showed up wild and complicated.

And later, much later, KB. Who never once asked me to be good, to be quiet, to be less.

But before him, there were plenty who tried.

...

There's a cost to rejecting the "good" girl narrative. Refuse to play along, and suddenly you're abrasive. Intimidating. Too much.

I had a boss. The kind of man who called women "girls" and expected them to smile at jokes that weren't jokes, just thinly veiled hostility disguised as humor (which is only funny when I do it). In meetings, he'd interrupt mid-sentence, talk over me like background noise, then present my ideas as his own with the confidence of someone who'd never been called out for intellectual theft.

The breaking point came during a staff meeting in the conference room. The coffee was burnt, Jim's ego was inflated, and I was about to lose my shit.

Jim sat at the head of the table, dispensing wisdom about a client project I'd been leading for months. The kind of wisdom lifted straight from the strategy document I'd emailed him the night before.

I watched him deliver my recommendations, word for word, while the rest of the team nodded at "his" insight. My research. My late nights. "His" brilliant idea.

He was really warming to his theme now, gesturing expansively as he explained concepts I'd spent weeks developing. The audacity was breathtaking.
When I opened my mouth to speak, he held up a hand and kept talking.

I'd had enough.

"Actually, Jim," I said, loud enough that everyone turned to look, "that's exactly what I was trying to tell you before you cut me off. I'm glad you like my idea."

Jim's face flushed red, a satisfying shade of humiliation.

That afternoon, he called me into his office.

"You embarrassed me," he said, his voice carrying that particular blend of wounded ego and administrative authority that mediocre men wield like a weapon.

I didn't even flinch. "You did that all by yourself."

He didn't like that. Called me difficult. Said I wasn't a "team player."

Translation: I wasn't playing by his rules.

Jim wasn't the only one who had a problem with me.
A client complained.
I was "too assertive."
I corrected him too often.

Translation: I had the audacity to be right while female.

My manager called me in. Asked me to explain myself.
As if the problem was honesty, not ego.

And in that moment, I knew: I was done contorting myself. Done apologizing. Done pretending to be less so men like Jim and my client could feel like more.

So, I quit. Walked away.
It felt brave. And a little like revenge.

Like a middle finger in a glitter cannon.

The myth of the "good" girl isn't just about being nice. It's about being compliant. It's about being small.

...

Small feels safe.

I get mistaken for harmless all the time. People see the size and assume softness. Assume I'm manageable. Containable. Easily dismissed.

What they don't realize is I specialize in making people regret their assumptions. I'm a double shot of espresso at the exact wrong moment. Bold. Ill-advised. Impossible to ignore.

I've learned to let people misread me. Let them project their comfortable narratives onto my deceptive exterior. Let them mistake my silence for compliance, my stillness for submission. It makes the destruction more satisfying when I'm the reason conversations stop mid-sentence and rooms go suddenly, beautifully quiet.

At a literary conference, I attended a panel where a pretentious author, the kind who wears scarves indoors and refers to his "body of work" without irony, dismissed every question from women with the kind of thinly veiled contempt that passes for intellectual superiority in certain circles. Each response dripping with condescension wrapped in academic jargon, as if speaking slowly enough might help our delicate feminine brains catch up to his towering intellect.

I watched him perform this little show for forty-five minutes, cataloging his arrogance like evidence for a case I was already building.

During the Q&A, I raised my hand. He pointed to me with that look. The one that said, *this should be quick and painless*. He was probably expecting something about character development or plot structure that he could deflect with a patronizing smile and a recommendation to read more widely.

That's the thing about men like him. They only calibrate threat in decibels and inches. Loud voices and broad shoulders register as danger. Quiet women who take notes? We're furniture with questions.

I asked a question that exposed the glaring contradictions in his work, quoting his own writing back to him with surgical precision. Line by line. Page by page. A dismantling disguised as curiosity.

That special kind of silence that follows public intellectual evisceration settled over the room.

He stammered something about "interesting perspective" while visibly sweating through his blazer, his carefully constructed authority crumbling in real time.

Afterward, a well-known editor pulled me aside. "I've waited three years to see someone do that," she whispered. "He never saw it coming."

Men like him rarely do.
Not when the knife looks like a question.

...

That moment wasn't an outlier. It was a pattern.
I've spent my life watching people try to fit into boxes
that were never built for them.
I've seen what it costs. I've paid it.
I've felt the backlash for choosing not to conform.
But the backlash was always worth it, because I'd rather
be true to myself than quiet for someone else's comfort.

The way I was raised taught me that respect mattered,
but it also taught me to respect myself.
I don't owe anyone smaller. I don't owe anyone softer.

Being good wasn't making anyone happy.
It wasn't making me happy.
It wasn't even making me good.
It was just making me invisible.

And I'm not here to be a ghost in my own life.

...

My mother and I are tangled in the most complex of
dances.

She tells me I'm too loud, too opinionated, too much,
while being all those things herself. She criticizes my
boundaries while having none of her own. She sighs
when I make waves, then creates tsunamis without
apology.

"Must you always make waves?" she asks.

Always. Because the alternative is drowning quietly
while everyone compliments your technique.

Which is the strangest part about my mom. She's a force herself. Never met a rule she didn't question, a boundary she didn't consider optional. She does exactly what she wants, consequences be damned.

But somehow, she expects differently from me. As if there are two rulebooks: one for her, one for her daughter. As if the freedom she claims for herself is somehow inappropriate for me to seize.

I used to think it was hypocrisy, pure and simple. The classic "do as I say, not as I do" that parents have been wielding since the beginning of time.

But it's more complicated than that. She respects when I stand up to the world, but bristles when I stand up to her. She admires my backbone until it stiffens against her own wishes. She taught me to say no to others, then seems surprised when I say no to her.

"I just want you to have an easier life than I did," she says when I challenge her expectations.

There's truth in those words, but not the whole truth. Beneath them lies a more complex reality: she wants me to be strong, but not strong enough to resist her. To be independent, but not independent from her. To be fierce, but only in the directions she approves.

It's the contradiction we live in. The push and pull between autonomy and connection, respect and control. Between two women who are, in many ways, too similar to peacefully coexist and too connected to walk away.

It took me years to understand that my mother's contradictions come from love, however imperfectly expressed. She doesn't want to control me so much as protect me, from heartbreak, from disappointment, from a world that hasn't always been kind to women like us.

The difference between us isn't just about boundaries. It's about duty. My mother is dutiful in ways I've never been. She fulfills obligations without questioning whether they should exist in the first place. She shows up, she delivers, she meets expectations, even as she complains about them.

I question the obligations themselves. I ask why before I say yes. I consider my own needs before others' expectations. In her eyes, this makes me selfish. In mine, it makes me sane.

She doesn't understand that the very strength I use to fight the world's expectations comes from her. That her defiance lives in my blood. That every time I refuse to dim my light, I'm honoring the part of her that refused to disappear.

I see her watching me sometimes, pride and fear warring in her eyes. Pride that I stand firm. Fear that the world will break me for it.

"You're like your father," she says. It lands like a diagnosis, not a compliment. An observation tinged with resentment. As if his DNA explains every refusal, every resistance. As if defiance is hereditary. And I'm proof.

But I'm like her too. In ways neither of us fully acknowledges.
The stubbornness. The fierce protection of those we love. The refusal to be defined by others' expectations. Her love demands sacrifice, the kind she's made her entire life.
Mine refuses to sacrifice authenticity, even at the cost of comfort.
Her love says, *I will give up anything for you.*
Mine says, *I will be true to myself for you.*

Both types of love can wound.
Both can heal.
Both come from a place of deep conviction.

My mother carries the weight of immigrant determination. The responsibility to build a new life in a foreign land. The pressure to justify her own sacrifices through stability, through success. Through raising a daughter who could navigate an American world while honoring Iranian roots.

As first-generation, born of Iranian parents but raised American, I stand on the bridge she built. But I'm not bound by the same obligations that defined her journey.

She internalized rules I've chosen to question. Accepted burdens I've refused to carry. Found ways to work within systems I prefer to dismantle.

And maybe that's the root of our tension. She bent to survive. I refuse to bend, even if it costs me.
She sees my resistance as recklessness. I see her bending as unnecessary surrender.

I love her. But I won't be that version of myself. Not even for her.

Not because I don't value her wisdom or respect her journey.
But because the greatest gift she ever gave me was the strength to choose my own path. Even when that path leads away from her carefully constructed protection. Even when it means being worse in her eyes, to be true in my own.

Our relationship exists in that tension. Between her fear and my freedom. Between her protection and my defiance. Between what she sacrificed and what I refuse to give up.

It's messy. Complicated. Sometimes painful.
But it's real. And in a world that constantly asks women to be simple, to be easy, to be less.
I'll take real over comfortable any day.
Even with my mother.
Especially with my mother.

We clash not because we're too different, but because we're too alike in all the wrong ways and too different in all the important ones.
Two strong women who never learned to yield, trying to love each other without compromising themselves in the process.

And somehow, we manage it.
Imperfectly. Painfully. Beautifully.

Because beneath all our differences, there's a truth we both know but rarely say: we are mirrors.

Reflecting different angles of the same fierce light.
The light that illuminates the expectations that have
shaped us both.

Mother and daughter.
Immigrant and first-generation.
Two women separated by culture and time.
United by the burden of being "good."

...

The myth of the "good" girl isn't just a myth. It's a
weapon.

I broke the cycle for myself. Now I break it for my son,
Grayson. Even at his young age, the world is already
trying to shape him, to tell him who he should be. But I
want him to know that he doesn't have to be "good" to
be loved. That he can be wild and loud and completely
himself, and it will never make me love him less. (Even
if I occasionally fantasize about boarding school.)

I want him to know that there's more power in
authenticity than in obedience. That the most
revolutionary act is to be exactly who you are, even
when the world is telling you to be someone else.

I want him to know what my dad taught me: that some
rules are meant to be broken. That some expectations
are meant to be defied.

That sometimes, staying yourself is the quietest
rebellion with the loudest consequences.

...

I think about Mrs. Peterson sometimes. Wonder if she's still out there telling little girls to be quiet, to be good, to care more about others than themselves.

I think about all the teachers and bosses and friends and lovers who expected me to fold, to soften, to sand down everything sharp and wild until I was smooth and easy to handle.

I think about the version of myself I might have become if I'd listened to them. If I'd believed that my worth was in my ability to make others comfortable.

And I'm so fucking grateful that I didn't.

I was learning, even then, that authenticity would always matter more than approval.

That living truthfully, even when labeled "worse" for it, was the only path I could walk.

...

I was never good at being good. But I was excellent at being real. Honest. Authentic. Unapologetically myself. Everything they warned me would make me unlovable.

And maybe that's a different kind of good. Maybe that's the kind that actually matters.

Not the artificial sweetness of a woman who's learned to swallow her truth to be tolerable.

But the messy, beautiful good of a woman who refuses to be anything but exactly who she is.

Even when it means being worse.

Especially when it means being worse.

I am the kind of worse that makes men shift in meetings, feeling their power slip. The kind of worse that walks into a room and doesn't ask for permission to exist. The kind of worse that refuses to soften her voice or her opinions. The kind of worse that calls out bullshit in real time instead of complaining about it later. The kind of worse that makes people uncomfortable because I represent everything they're afraid to be themselves.

A sweet girl like me was never meant to be crazy, but unfortunately I am.

I am the kind of worse that doesn't save her rage for private moments.
I let it breathe.
I let it show up in my book.
I let it be seen.

I'm done aspiring to their version of good.

It was never about goodness. It was about being compliant.

And I'd rather be worse than controlled any day.

unlearning the rules

I didn't wear white after Labor Day. I spooned my soup away from me. I always brought a gift when visiting someone's home for the first time.

I was excellent at performance. Terrible at compliance. Turns out there's a difference between knowing your lines and believing in the play.

I could follow the etiquette rules perfectly. It's the bigger ones I couldn't swallow. The ones that required me to shrink, to stay quiet, to be less.

I learned these rules the way children learn gravity. Through repeated impact. The world taught me its expectations one uncomfortable silence at a time. One raised eyebrow. One "well, that's…interesting" delivered with the emotional temperature of a morgue.

I always knew the rules. I just never wanted to follow them. So I mimicked. I marched to their beat in costume, but never in spirit. When you grow up surrounded by rules, you internalize their rhythm. Even when you're marching to your own beat, you're still keeping time.

I didn't escape unscathed. I contorted. I overthought. I wondered if being too much was the reason I was never enough.

Eventually, I realized that the rules weren't just limiting. They were suffocating.

...

I remember the first rule I learned to follow. I must have been four, maybe five. A family gathering, crowded with adults whose names I couldn't keep straight. I was bored, restless, craving attention.

"Shirin," my mother whispered, kneeling to my level. "Be a good girl and play quietly. Adults are talking."

It was the first of many versions of that instruction. Be quiet. Be good. Be less.

I tried. I rehearsed the quiet. I attempted the smallness. I practiced invisibility.

But something in me always rebelled. Some wild, untamed part that refused to be silenced, minimized, to be less than what I was meant to be.

My father saw it. Recognized it. Nurtured it, even. "You've got fire," he'd tell me, when my mother wasn't listening. "Don't let anyone put it out."

But the world has so many ways of extinguishing flames.

...

Breaking the Workplace Rules

The timelines blur. The workplace stories weave together across time, across buildings with identical fluorescent lighting. Companies bleed into one another. I've changed names, altered settings, smudged identifying details to protect myself from corporate revenge. But every emotional truth stands untouched. The lessons remain intact. The wisdom honestly earned.

My first lesson in workplace rebellion came early. I was managing a restaurant when this woman walked in, wearing sunglasses indoors, and immediately started snapping her fingers at me like I was a disobedient Labrador.

"You. Girl." Not ma'am. Not excuse me. Just "girl," delivered with the authority of someone who'd clearly never worked a service job in her life. "I need my order taken now. And don't screw it up like last time."

Last time? I'd never seen this woman before in my life, but apparently I was responsible for every restaurant disappointment she'd ever experienced.

I smiled the way women do when they're deciding between customer service and homicide, that special grimace that says I'm about to choose violence but it'll be polite violence. "Coming right up," I said, then paused long enough to let the anticipation build. "Just one question: Did your parents teach you to speak to people like personal servants, or is that a skill you developed on your own?"

The restaurant got very, very quiet. The kind of quiet where every patron suddenly finds their salad fascinating while straining to catch every word. Even the kitchen staff peeked through the window, probably wondering if they should start recording or call security.

"Excuse me?" she sputtered, her sunglasses sliding down her nose to reveal eyes wide with the shock of someone who'd never been challenged by "the help."

"Oh, I can repeat it slower if that helps," I offered with the overly patient tone of someone providing customer service. Just not the kind she was expecting.

She left in a huff, but called the owner the next day with a theatrical retelling where I'd apparently threatened her life rather than her ego.

The owner asked me if this was true. This was my chance to lie, to pretend, to take the safe route.

Instead: "I asked her if her parents taught her to be rude or if she came up with it herself. Technically a question, not a threat."

I was fired by the end of the week. The official reason: "rude and abusive behavior toward customers." The unofficial reason: I broke the sacred covenant that the customer's dignity matters more than mine.

It was worth it. Some bridges deserve to be burned, especially the ones that require you to crawl across them.

...

There's a very specific choreography expected of women in the workplace. You need to speak your mind without actually having one. Be confident enough to contribute, deferential enough to disappear. Smile, but not like you mean it. Have opinions, but package them as suggestions.

I tried to walk that tightrope for years, but I'm not great at pretending. I'm assertive. I'm opinionated. And I'm not interested in sugarcoating my ideas just to make them easier for people who need flattery more than facts. I was never built for subtle.

Standing up to Jim in that staff meeting felt like a victory. Until I realized he was just the prelude.

One client refused to acknowledge anything I contributed. He'd talk over me in meetings, ignore my input, and only respond when my male colleagues repeated what I had just said. Same words, different delivery system.

It was the kind of infuriating dismissal that makes you fantasize about flipping a conference table. Or just slowly sliding off your chair and playing dead. Or starting every sentence with "As Jim was about to say..." The meetings felt endless, like trying to breathe in a room where the air was thicker with ego than oxygen.

I could handle the disrespect. I'd done that dance before.
But things got worse when my integrity became the sacrifice they expected.
A client requested something blatantly illegal. Not questionable. Not unethical. *Illegal.*

I refused.

Suddenly, I wasn't just assertive. I was insubordinate.

It should have been simple. But my manager, a former surfer kid turned corporate yes-man, didn't see it that way. He was the type of guy who thought charisma was a substitute for competence. He'd surfed his way to the top, all sun-bleached smiles and empty promises, and couldn't understand why I wouldn't just go along.

"But the client asked for it," he said, leaning back in his chair like this was just another harmless conversation about deliverables, not felony risk. "It's fine."

"Oh, cool. So, if the client asks me to murder someone, and I'm on trial, I'll just say, 'But they asked me to.' That'll hold up in court."

He blinked. Like I'd suggested a blood ritual instead of basic legal compliance. He wasn't concerned about the felony part, only that I'd made things awkward. What mattered was keeping the client happy. And in his mind, I was the problem. Difficult. Noncompliant. Uncooperative.

Ethics weren't the priority.

I wasn't either.

How dare I make it uncomfortable by telling the truth.

It blew up, of course. Because that's what happens when a woman stands her ground and refuses to compromise her integrity. It becomes "a situation." Not because I was wrong, but because I wasn't willing to be quiet about being right.

The rules were clear: say yes, look agreeable, and stay quiet. But the game was never meant for me to win. Especially when the game wasn't about skill, but about who could nod along the hardest. My manager wasn't rewarded for competence. He was rewarded for saying yes with a smile and never asking the wrong questions, like, "Is this legal?" Apparently, integrity is a great trait unless you want to keep your job.

My manager called me into his office, face solemn.

"The client has been complaining about you," he said, as if delivering a terminal diagnosis.

I waited for the defense. The support. The acknowledgment that this particular client was known for his misogyny, for his resistance to women who dared to correct him when he was wrong.

It never came.

Instead, he asked me to explain myself. As if I were the problem. As if refusing to let a man walk all over me was somehow unprofessional.

He wanted remorse.

I gave him clarity.

In that moment, something snapped. Like a bone breaking along a line it had been tracing for years. A realization that had been forming suddenly locked into perfect clarity.

The rules would never protect me. They were never designed to. They existed to keep me in my place, to make sure I never became a threat. They were designed to tame me. That didn't work either. Just woman enough to be interesting, not enough to be dangerous.

The betrayal was surgical. Precise. One man dismissed my expertise, another questioned my response to it. The perfect circle of professional betrayal was complete. The ancient dance of men reinforcing each other's power while women are expected to smile and apologize for existing too loudly.

So, I quit. Walked away from that world of false meritocracy and unspoken expectations. And it felt like breaking the surface after being held underwater for too long.

Not reborn. Just finally unburdened.

...

I think about all the years I spent trying to play by rules that were rigged against me. All the hours I spent shape-shifting into whatever version felt safest: the "right" kind of woman, the "right" kind of professional, the "right" kind of human.

What could I have built with that energy? What mountains might I have moved? How many other books could I have written, each one a delicious act of revenge against the people who wronged me?

And then I had my son, and the cost became impossible to ignore.

Walking away from the corporate workplace wasn't just about prioritizing my family. It was about prioritizing myself. It was about unlearning the rules that told me I had to collapse inward to succeed.

...

Success doesn't always look like more. Sometimes it looks like less. Less noise. Less bullshit. Less pretending you're fine while your soul's plotting an escape.

Success is choosing a Monday that doesn't start with dread. It's eating lunch at a real table, not your lap, not the car, not wedged between back-to-back meetings like a hostage negotiating for fifteen minutes and a sandwich. It's talking to your kid without a calendar alert screaming over his voice. It's not crying in the Whole Foods parking lot because your Slack status says "available" and you are anything but.

Sometimes that means being "worse." Sometimes that means breaking the rules. And sometimes that means walking away from a game that was never meant for you to win.

I didn't fail the system. I just stopped cosplaying the version of me it could tolerate.

...

The hardest rules to unlearn are the ones you didn't even know you were following. The ones you never agreed to. The ones you absorbed before you had language. The ones so deeply ingrained that they feel like personality.

Like the rule that says motherhood should look a certain way. That "good" mothers should sacrifice everything for their children. Should smile through exhaustion. Should find martyrdom fulfilling.

Or the rule that says grief should be private, dignified, contained. That anything beyond one year is considered emotionally indulgent. That after a certain amount of time, you should be "over it." Moved on. Healed. Ideally without making anyone else uncomfortable.

These are the rules that live under our skin. The ones you absorb through cultural osmosis, through watching your mothers and grandmothers, through magazine articles and movies, and casual comments from strangers.

The invisible rules cut deepest. They pose as personal failures rather than social constraints.

...

Life doesn't come with instructions. And if it did, I'd probably have thrown them out of the car window by now. Most of what I've learned has come the hard way, through mistakes, moments of clarity, and more than a few "oh shit" realizations.

I used to think I could fix people. If I just loved them enough, supported them enough. What I didn't realize was that I wasn't responsible for anyone else's healing. I could hold space, but I couldn't carry their burdens for them.

I spent years in a relationship that felt less like dating and more like running tech support for someone else's nervous system. When he spiraled, I was there to pick up the pieces. When he lashed out, I told myself it wasn't personal. I thought my patience and love could fix him.

They didn't.

Because people don't work that way. They don't heal just because you want them to. They have to want it for themselves. Some people don't want to be understood. They just want to be enabled with an audience.

Unlearning the savior complex might've been the hardest rule to break. The one that said I was responsible for other people's happiness. Their healing. Their growth.

The one that said my worth was tied to what I could do for others rather than who I simply was.

Letting go isn't some graceful surrender. It's a fight. It's clawing pieces of yourself back from someone who never deserved them. You don't become some better version of yourself. You just stop pretending you were ever less than whole.

There was a moment, years later, when I looked back at that relationship with fresh eyes. I wasn't angry anymore. I wasn't bitter. I was just...sad. Sad for the girl who thought love was something she had to earn by sacrificing pieces of herself.

She didn't know better.

...

Grayson is watching me break every rule I was raised to follow.

He sees me refuse to shrink when people talk over me. He watches me walk away from jobs that demand my soul as payment. He's there when I choose honesty over politeness, authenticity over approval.

I'm not teaching him to rebel. I'm showing him what happens when you stop asking permission to exist.

The world will try to tame him too. Tell him to be good, to be quiet, to be less. But he's got a front-row seat to what happens when you refuse.

That's not a lesson plan. It's a live demonstration.

And demonstrations are so much more dangerous than lectures.

...

What does it feel like to unlearn the rules you've lived by? To shed the expectations that have shaped your choices, your dreams, your sense of what's possible?

It feels like grief. Sometimes. Mourning the years spent trying to be someone you never were. The energy wasted on fitting into spaces too small for your soul.

It feels like anger. Often. Fury at the systems that profited from your compliance. At the people who enforced rules they themselves didn't follow. At yourself, for believing it for so long.

It feels like vertigo. Like stepping off a cliff and realizing you've been wearing wings all along. Terrifying and exhilarating in equal measure.

But mostly, it feels like finding the person you were always meant to be beneath the layers of "should" and "must" and "appropriate."

Like taking off your bra at the end of a long day.

Necessary.
Relieving.
Almost holy.

...

I don't have all the rules unlearned yet. There are still moments I catch myself fading, apologizing, trying to fit.

The patterns of my past cling like smoke to clothes. Familiar. Persistent. Even when I've opened all the windows. Even when I know better, they cling.

Every day, I get a little worse. The kind of worse that makes people shift uncomfortably in their seats. The kind of worse that spreads like wildfire once someone sees it's possible.

Every day, I break another rule. Question another assumption. Shed another expectation.

Some days I toe the line.
Others, I redraw it entirely.
And every time I do, the air clears.

I write honestly about the messy, difficult parts of life because sanitized stories serve no one except those invested in maintaining the status quo. If it costs me friendships? Those connections were just comfortable lies we were telling each other anyway. That's what makes it worse. And better.

I don't pretend to be interested in conversations that only revolve around surface-level topics. I let the silence hang in the air instead of filling it with polite chatter. I want the real stuff. Childhood damage. The things that broke you. The lessons you learned the hard way. The things that left a mark.

Tell me about your trauma. I don't care what you do for work. What's the worst thing you've done to someone you love? Tell me about the guy you dated in high school and why your mom and aunt aren't speaking.

I refuse to nod along just because it's what everyone else is doing. I challenge assumptions, even when it makes people uncomfortable. The discomfort is the point.

I prioritize my joy, my health, my sense of self, even when society tells me good mothers should give up everything.

The worse I get by society's standards, the more dangerous I become.

The kind of worse that terrifies the rule-makers because they know once enough of us stop playing by their rules, the game is over.

And with every rule broken, every expectation shattered, I become a little more myself.

A little more worse.
A little more free.
And somehow, more whole.

everything after

My dad died in 2012. I remember the date, the time, the way his room smelled of antiseptic and endings. The strange weightlessness of his hand in mine. The slight stubble on his cheeks because no one had thought to shave him that morning. The absolute silence that followed his last breath, as if the universe itself had paused to acknowledge his passing.

I thought I knew what grief would look like. I'd seen it in movies, read about it in books. The initial shock. The funeral. The period of mourning. And then, eventually, the return to life. Changed, certainly. Scarred, undoubtedly. But fundamentally moved forward.

I expected the five stages they promise you: denial, anger, bargaining, depression, acceptance. What I got instead was more like thirty-seven stages, including "crying in public restrooms," "accidentally calling his number at 2am," and my personal favorite, "tattooing my name in his handwriting even though he would've absolutely hated it, just to spite his absence." Nobody warns you about that stage. They don't sell greeting cards for it.

...

A month after my dad died, I was invited to a friend's wedding. I shouldn't have gone. I was still raw, still randomly bursting into tears when a song that reminded me of him played.

During the reception, some random woman cornered me, champagne sloshing dangerously close to my dress as she leaned in. "So what does your father do?"

A normal person would have said "He passed away recently" and accepted the appropriate sympathetic noises. Instead, I looked her straight in the eye and said, "Currently? Decomposing."

Her champagne stopped mid-air. Her mouth opened and closed like a fish.

"I'm sorry, that was inappropriate," I said, not sorry at all. "The technically correct answer is that he's being cremated next week, so soon he'll be doing whatever ashes do. Probably getting accidentally vacuumed."

He wasn't even getting cremated. We'd buried him days after he died. But something in me couldn't resist twisting the knife, making her as uncomfortable as possible for asking such a mundane question during the least mundane period of my life.

The woman fled, likely telling everyone what a terrible person I was. (Valid.) But grief doesn't come with a politeness filter. It doesn't follow social scripts. It doesn't care about wedding reception etiquette.

I laughed so hard in the bathroom afterward that I nearly threw up. The kind of laughter that's one molecule away from sobbing. The kind that would horrify grief counselors everywhere. The kind that felt more honest than all the "he's in a better place" bullshit I'd been choking on for weeks.

My dad would have loved that story. Would have laughed that full-body laugh that made strangers turn and smile without knowing why. Would have said, "That's my girl" with that specific mix of pride and mischief I'll never hear again.

Some losses don't fit into polite conversation. Some pain doesn't translate into acceptable small talk. Some loves are too big to be discussed properly at a stranger's wedding.

That wedding reinforced everything wrong with the grief industry's favorite lie. Those five neat stages I'd already discovered were bullshit? Turns out the world expects you to perform them properly. As if grief were a road trip with clearly marked destinations. As if you could check them off one by one until you reach the final stop: healed. What they don't tell you is how you'll cycle through them all in a single afternoon. How you'll wake up in acceptance only to be plunged into denial by the sound of a voicemail you forgot to delete. How years later, when you think you've settled comfortably into your new normal, a song or a smell will drag you back to bargaining as if no time has passed at all.

That champagne-soaked reception taught me lesson one: grief forces honesty in a world full of pleasant fiction.

...

Three months after my dad died, I was standing alone at a gas station, staring at the pump like I'd never seen one before.

He never let me pump gas when he was around. Even a few days out from surgery, bandaged and limping, he insisted on getting out to do it himself. I was driving him home from the hospital, and before I could stop him, he was already at the pump. Like nothing could keep him from taking care of me. Not even pain.

I didn't realize how much I'd taken it for granted until that moment. How much it wasn't about the gas. It was about being loved in the smallest, most consistent ways. Someone who made my comfort his job. Someone who loved me enough to make sure my hands never smelled like unleaded.

I broke down next to pump seven. Ugly, heaving sobs while some teenager at the next pump pretended not to notice.

Pump seven taught me lesson two: grief lives in your muscle memory. In all the small kindnesses you never thought to name until they disappeared.

...

I found myself standing in grocery store aisles, staring at his favorite foods, paralyzed by the realization I no longer needed to buy them.
Such a small thing.
Such an enormous thing.

Aisle three taught me lesson three: grief isn't just the tear-soaked pillow from sad movies. It's also inappropriate laughter at funerals, sex with people you don't care about (because orgasms shut off your brain for five minutes), and buying ridiculous things online at 3am because any dopamine hit is better than despair. It's the absolutely mundane reality that you still have to take out the trash and pay your phone bill while everything inside you is screaming.

It lives in your body. It wakes you at strange hours, not with tears but with the sudden urge to rearrange your entire kitchen or book a flight to somewhere you've never been. The way it makes you both numb and hypersensitive all at once.

Grief is that moment when someone asks "How are you?" and you almost tell them the truth. Almost let slip that you've been wearing the same outfit for three days because laundry feels impossible. That you forget how to breathe when a certain song plays. That even the quiet sounds like betrayal.

But you don't say any of that.

You say "I'm fine" because the world has no patience for grief that outlasts the funeral.

Grief speaks in truths no one wants to hear. I became an expert at translation. At turning "I found another voicemail from him I hadn't deleted and it broke me for two days" into "I'm just tired." At converting "I'm still not sure how to exist in a world where he doesn't" into "Taking it one day at a time." I learned to lie in fluent small talk.

The world wanted my grief packaged neatly. Resolved by the first anniversary. Transformed into inspirational memes by the second.

But grief doesn't know about timelines. It doesn't check the calendar before showing up in the pasta aisle or during a Tuesday meeting, or while you're finally having good sex again.

It just arrives. Unannounced. Unwelcome. Undeniable.

And you learn to make room for it. To live alongside it.

...

What I didn't expect was how grief would ambush me years later, in the most ordinary moments.

Like when Grayson was born. My first thought wasn't gratitude or relief. It was: my dad will never hold him. Joy and grief showed up together, neither one willing to wait its turn.

The nurse thought my tears were from pain or joy. The usual suspects. She didn't understand I was experiencing a death and a birth simultaneously. The arrival of my son and the fresh loss of my father, who should have been there to welcome him.

Or the first time Grayson laughed. A sound so pure and perfect it seemed to exist outside of time. My immediate thought wasn't just delight at this milestone. It was: I need to call Dad. He would love this.

Then the crushing remembrance: I can't call Dad. I'll never call Dad again.

Grief learned new ways to show up as Grayson grew. It wasn't just missing my father as I had known him. It was mourning the grandfather he would have been. The relationship they would have had. The parts of my father I'd never get to see emerge in this new role.

And grief brought guilt along with it. Guilt that these moments of sadness were intruding on what should be purely joyful experiences. Guilt that I was somehow tainting Grayson's childhood with the shadow of a loss he would never understand. Guilt that some part of me was absent even as I tried to be fully present with my son.

But my father was there anyway. In the determined set of Grayson's jaw. In my instincts, shaped by hands I can't hold anymore. In the way grief and love refuse to exist separately, no matter how much easier that would be.

Grayson calls KB "baba" now. The same Persian word I used for my father since childhood. Every time I hear it, something ancient and wounded in me exhales. Maybe he does know this part of me. Maybe love finds its way forward in the language we keep.

There were days when I'd catch a glimpse of my father in Grayson. A particular expression. A stubborn tilt of the head. A way of concentrating on a task that was so familiar it made my heart stop.

"He's just like you," friends would say, watching him explain why the rules don't apply to him specifically.

But I'd see my dad in him and think: No, he's just like someone he never got to meet. Someone who would have called him *jaanam*. Someone who would have let him be exactly what he was without trying to fix any of it. Someone who would have met him at full volume and said, *You're mine. I know exactly what kind of boy you are.*

There were nights I'd dream of them together. My father teaching Grayson about physics or basketball or the precise way to make the perfect cup of tea. Dreams so vivid I'd wake up convinced, for one disorienting moment, that my father was still alive. That he was just in the other room with my son.

The crash back to reality was always brutal. Like losing him twice.

KB found me once at 3 AM, silent tears streaming down my face as I scrolled through old photos of my dad on my phone.

"I just wanted to see his face," I explained, though KB hadn't asked. "I keep thinking I'm forgetting what his voice sounded like."

He sat down beside me, his shoulder pressed against mine. Didn't try to fix it. Didn't try to cheer me up. Just existed with me in that moment of grief.

"Tell me about him," he said. "Tell me something Grayson should know someday."

So I did.

I told him how my dad had the kind of sense of humor that left you unsure whether you were in on the joke or the target. How anyone who dared park in front of his house somehow ended up with a flat tire. Always a nail. Always a mystery. And how, after he died, we found a giant bucket of nails in the garage. "Coincidence," he would've said, completely deadpan.

How he left all the activation stickers on his credit cards. His theory: if someone stole them, they'd assume the cards weren't active and wouldn't bother trying to use them. Airtight logic. Except he had to explain it to every cashier who thought he was handing them an unusable card.

How he could fix almost anything but created twice as many problems just for the thrill of it.

Somehow, sharing those stories with KB made the grief feel less like a hole and more like a thread. Like maybe if I kept telling them, my dad would keep existing. Through KB. Through Grayson. Through every tire that still holds air.

As Grayson gets older, I catch myself telling him stories about his grandfather that I've...edited. Polished.

Sanitized for child consumption. But other days, I tell him the real versions. The ones with splinters.

About how his grandfather once got us kicked out of a museum for arguing with the physics exhibit. How he'd challenge police officers with questions like "at what velocity do you allege I was traveling?" while I sank lower in the passenger seat, mortified, impressed, and already drafting his eulogy.

The obituary called him "a respected engineer." It should have said "magnificent troublemaker who could explain quantum physics to a five-year-old and still lose his keys three times a week."

Not every bridge is meant to burn. Some are built by grief and held together by memory and sheer stubborn love.
He's not here in the traditional sense, but he's present.
In the values.
In the fingerprints he left on me, now smudged into the next generation.

Grief, I've learned, isn't something you get over. It's something you get better at carrying. Sometimes it's a boulder you drag behind you. Sometimes it's a pebble in your shoe. Sometimes, on rare, precious days, it's light enough to hold without wincing. To sit with, not in pain, but in acceptance. Quiet. Unwelcome. Still mine.

But it never disappears. It shifts. Morphs. Becomes the quiet hum underneath everything else. And on good days, it feels less like pain and more like proof. That they mattered. That they *still* matter.

Grief is love with nowhere to go. But it goes somewhere anyway. Into memory. Into story. Into the quiet ways we still say their name.

Grayson will know his grandfather. Through the way I parent, shaped by how I was parented. Through inappropriate jokes, stubborn opinions, and a complete disregard for authority when it deserves to be questioned.

It's not enough. It will never be enough.

But it's what grief has taught me to make of an impossible loss. Make it a tether. A bridge between what was and what is. A way of carrying the dead with me into the future they'll never see.

Not with acceptance. But with the kind of love that refuses to be limited by something as mundane as death.

...

Grief doesn't rush. It just waits. Silently. Relentlessly. Until you stop trying to outpace it.

You sit with it. Or it sits on you.

When my dad was dying, my uncle told me to "be strong."
What he meant was: *Don't cry in front of your dad.*
Don't let him see how much it's breaking you.
Don't make his dying about your pain.

Be quiet. Be useful. Be less.

But I've never been good at pretending I wasn't shattered.
And I don't think silence is strength.

Strength is letting it wreck you. And still showing up. Not polished. Not composed. Just there.

...

I remember the last good day.

My father in a hospital bed, tucked into a space that used to feel like his refuge. The familiar walls of his bedroom now transformed by medical equipment. The space that had always been his sanctuary now feeling both intimate and clinical at once.

He was lucid that day. Present. His eyes clear for the first time in weeks.

We talked about books. About physics. About Albert Einstein, one of his heroes. About sinusoidal waves, how he saw relationships not as rollercoasters like most people would say, but as mathematical curves with predictable patterns of ups and downs.

A mad scientist till the very end.

Then, in the middle of explaining a concept I only half understood, he reached for my hand. His fingers felt like paper, fragile and thin, the bones too close to the surface.

"Shirin," he said, my name soft in his mouth. "When I'm gone, don't let them tell you how to miss me."

I didn't understand then what he meant. I do now.

He knew what was coming. Not just his death, but the after. The well-meaning advice. The cultural expectations. The friends who would expect me to "move on" in tidy, predictable ways.

He knew I would grieve loudly, messily, in ways that made others uncomfortable. And he was giving me permission.

It was the last lesson he taught me. The most important one.

...

Grief taught me that love doesn't end with death. It just changes shape, slipping into the quiet moments when you least expect it.

It lingers in memories, in the empty chair at the table, and in the unanswered calls I still catch myself making, reaching for a voice that will never answer again. It taught me that the people we lose don't really leave us, they stay with us, in the memories we carry, in what we pass down, and the ways they shaped us.

Grief also taught me to let go of the need to be "good." Because what does it even mean to be a "good" mourner? Wear black, say the right words, and cry exactly the right amount, but not too much, because that makes people uncomfortable. As if grief comes with a dress code and a script.

If that's "good," I guess I failed spectacularly.

I didn't have to be the stoic daughter, the strong niece, or the perfect mourner. I just had to be me, messy, broken, and human.

...

Loss strips you down to the essentials. Not appearances or performing grief for others, but honoring the relationship in whatever way feels true.

Sometimes that means breaking the rules. Crying when you're told to be strong. Speaking the truth when silence is easier.

My culture taught me that strength meant hiding heartache. But real strength isn't about how well you can hide it. It's about how bravely you can face it.

The funeral. The sea of black. The rhythmic wailing of relatives I barely knew. The whispers about propriety. About tradition.

My mother, still and silent, grief locked behind her eyes.

My brother across the room, our eyes meeting in moments of shared understanding. He didn't want to speak at the funeral. Couldn't. Words failed him in his grief, and why shouldn't they?

But our uncle kept pressuring him, even on the day of the service. "You're the son. You should say something," he insisted, his voice carrying that familiar tone of authority that expected immediate compliance. As if grief came with obligations based on gender and birth order. As if my brother's silence wasn't its own tribute to a father who didn't always follow the rules, and never asked us to be anyone we weren't.

I stepped between them, feeling something primal rise in my chest. The room seemed to narrow, faces turning toward the impending scene.

I could feel the weight of tradition, or propriety, of centuries of "proper mourning" pressing against my skin.

"He doesn't have to do anything," I said, voice low, but carrying. Not a whisper, I wanted witnesses. "Leave him alone."

My uncle's face registered shock before hardening into disapproval. The scandal of a woman interrupting ritual. The horror of grief expressed without rules. I saw relatives' eyes widen. Silent pleas for peace on this, of all days. But peace had never been my specialty. And my father, the man whose body lay just feet away, had never asked me for peace. He had asked for truth.

It caused a scene. The kind of scene you're not supposed to make at funerals. I could hear my uncle later, talking to my aunt. Snippets reached me: his voice, the specific register of disapproval. "Always difficult...thinks she knows better...disrespectful..."

The last thread of my composure snapped. I abandoned any pretense of politeness and moved toward where they stood, my grief transforming into something feral and unstoppable.

"This is my father's funeral," I said, not bothering to lower my voice. Let them all hear. Let them remember. "And you're standing here talking badly about his daughter instead of honoring him. *That's* what's disrespectful. Not me."

The look on his face. Shock collapsing into embarrassment, then hardening into anger. The twin realizations: that I had heard him, and that I would not pretend I hadn't. That even in grief, especially in grief, I would not play by rules that sought to tame me.

He stopped talking. But something had been revealed that could never be hidden again. Even in our darkest moments, some people will try to police how we feel, how we express ourselves, how we honor what we've lost.

And me? I was sobbing openly. Messily. Without restraint. Exactly as my father would have expected. Exactly as I needed to.

...

But grief didn't just show me how to carry loss. It showed me who was willing to carry it with me.

Some people weren't.

My friends, the ones I thought would be there, struggled with my grief. They told me I had changed, like it was a flaw, like grief should leave you untouched and identical. What they meant was, "Be who you were before. Be easier for us."

But I wasn't.

They didn't want me to change, they wanted me to snap back into the version of myself that didn't make them uncomfortable. The version that laughed easily, stayed light, and didn't remind them of life's fragility.

People start avoiding you like grief might be contagious. Like if they stand too close, death might notice them too. They stop inviting you places because you're suddenly this walking reminder of mortality, this human memento mori ruining perfectly good cocktail parties with your inconvenient emotional reality. I wanted to wear a t-shirt: "Relax, I'm not going to mention my dead father. Unless your small talk is really fucking boring, then all bets are off."

But grief isn't a cold you can catch. It's demolition and reconstruction. It rips through your foundation and forces you to rebuild on shaky ground, with no blueprint and nothing guaranteed to hold.

It rewires you in ways that make others uncomfortable, especially those who prefer their pain behind closed doors.

They wanted grief to be like bad weather, brief and distant, something they could acknowledge from behind the safety of a window. But grief wasn't a storm I could wait out. It was a flood, and I was drowning.

It leaves you fumbling through a world that feels suddenly unfamiliar. You don't laugh the same. You don't love the same. You don't even breathe the same.

Grief stitches you back together with rough, mismatched seams, like a patchwork done in the dark.

Nothing fits the same. Some parts are too tight, some are missing entirely, and you're left wondering if you'll ever feel whole again, or if wholeness was just an illusion to begin with.

They wanted me to be the kind of person who could grieve quietly, privately, the kind who didn't force them to confront their own fear of loss. But if you can't sit with my grief, how could you ever sit with your own?

Grief transforms you. It's supposed to. Growth is born from pain. The ones who couldn't sit with my sadness? They'll never grow. They're allergic to discomfort. I stopped shrinking for people afraid of depth.

...

I remember the first time I laughed after my dad died. Really laughed, the kind that bubbles up from somewhere deep and surprises you with its intensity.

It was just hours after he passed. The house still heavy with the presence of death. My brother and I, wandering through rooms that felt both familiar and foreign without our father in them.

We found something in his home. Something so perfectly, ridiculously *him* that it broke through the numbness. I don't even remember what it was now. Just that it sparked a memory, a story, some essence of who he had been.

And suddenly we were laughing. Both of us, laughing until tears came. Until we couldn't tell if we were laughing or crying or both.

In that moment, laughing and crying simultaneously in the house where our father had just died, I felt his presence so strongly it was almost physical. As if joy and pain together could somehow bridge the distance between life and death.

Grief built the bridge. I walked across it. And I realized: this is how I would carry him forward. Not in solemn remembrance or silent reverence, but in the messy, contradictory fullness of life. In laughter that turns to tears. In stories that keep him present. In choices that would make him proud.

...

Grief changed me permanently. Left me stripped down to something...elemental. Made me impatient with small talk and social niceties. Gave me an almost brutal clarity about what matters and what doesn't.

I lost friends because of it. People who wanted the before-version of me, the one who could pretend that death was something that happened to other people. The one who didn't know how quickly everything you love can disappear.

But I gained something too. A deeper appreciation for the people who could sit with my pain without trying to fix it or rush it or minimize it. A finely tuned bullshit detector. A capacity for joy that's somehow more intense because I know its opposite so intimately.

My dad's death divided my life into before and after. There's no going back to before. There's only learning to live in the after, carrying both the loss and the love forward.

...

In the end, I learned that grief isn't just about loss.
It's about love.
It's about what we choose to carry forward, and how we let it shape us.

Losing my dad broke me.
But it also remade me.
Into the kind of worse that refuses to grieve on someone else's schedule or terms.

If that kind of worse makes people uncomfortable, good.
Their discomfort is nothing compared to my loss.

I became the kind of worse that cried openly in public without apologizing.
The kind of worse that kept saying his name long after it made people squirm.
The kind of worse that refused to "move on" just to make casual acquaintances feel better about mortality.

The kind of worse that knows grief doesn't end.
It just changes form.

The kind of worse that knows anyone asking "aren't you over it yet?" has never loved deeply enough to understand what loss really means.

The kind of worse that honors grief instead of packaging it up for easier consumption.

The kind of worse that refused to slip back into a "normal" that no longer existed.

The kind of worse that isn't afraid to say his name, mention him in casual conversation, keep him present in a world that would rather forget the dead than face its own fear of ending.

I'm the kind of worse that makes people uncomfortable.
Because grief isn't supposed to last this long.
Or cut this deep.
Or remain this present.

I don't know that I want to move on.
The further I get from the pain, the further I get from him.
And maybe that's okay.
Maybe staying here, in this tender wounded place, is how I keep him close.

If that unsettles people, that says more about their fear than about my healing.

And I'd be worse all over again if I had to.
Because anything less would be a lie.

Being worse, refusing to downplay loss, is the only honest response to love that deep.

Love isn't about holding back.
It's about showing up, even when it hurts.
It's about letting it change you forever.

And if that kind of change makes me worse, then worse is exactly what I'll choose.

Worse means I survived.
Worse means I felt it all and didn't look away.

Worse means I loved my father so much that losing him rewrote the fabric of who I am.

I've stopped looking for the final stage of grief.
Stopped waiting to be "healed" or "over it."

Instead, I recognize my father in the spaces between breaths.
The conversations I still have with him while driving alone.
The questions I save for him, knowing they'll go unanswered but asking anyway.

This isn't closure.
This isn't moving on.

This is just what love looks like after someone leaves.

love, unfiltered

I 've never loved delicately.
I've loved like it was a dare,
or a debt,
or a diagnosis.

And I kept coming back like the lesson was going to change.

I've loved men who collected my vulnerabilities like baseball cards, and others who treated emotional intimacy like a communicable disease.

I've loved recklessly. Strategically.
Out of boredom. Out of spite.

I've loved people who deserved walk-on roles and gave them starring credits.

Dating isn't about finding love.

It's about discovering exactly how creative people can get with disappointment.

A masterclass in human psychology.
Where everyone's lying about their intentions.
Including you.

And I?
I was an excellent student.

...

Love wasn't supposed to find me in a coffee shop.

It wasn't supposed to start with eye contact that feels like a conversation.
Or stifled laughter at the obnoxiously loud guy sitting nearby.
It wasn't supposed to begin with a man who didn't even drink coffee, who slid into the seat beside me with a conspiratorial smile that made me immediately intrigued.

It wasn't supposed to be that easy.

But there was KB. Four hours disappeared. We were still talking. About everything. Nothing. Books and dreams and bad life choices, whether dogs are better than cats, and if we believed in fate.

Do I believe in fate? I didn't. Not until that day.

Not until that random choice to stop at that particular coffee shop, to sit at that particular table, when a man who didn't even like coffee decided to stop in.

Until KB.

...

Before him, there were others. So many others.

Not bad boys. Just broken ones.
Men who mistook volatility for depth.
Men who couldn't sit with their own pain, so they
handed it to me.

The dark-haired, blue-eyed screw-up.
The boy with tattoos instead of morals.
The alcoholic who spiraled faster than I could anchor
him.

I called them lessons.
I didn't learn them.

All of them: charming, chaotic, always a crisis.
They filled my days with turbulence and distraction.

The alcoholic made a full-time job out of self-sabotage.
We spent a tumultuous stretch rehashing his
professional disappointments and pretending we were
building a life.
Really, I was building his spine for him.
Therapist. Cheerleader. Backup generator.

He talked about our future like it was inevitable. Grand,
loud, and entirely dependent on me carrying the
emotional load. He painted it in broad, intoxicating
strokes. But when my dad was diagnosed with cancer,
the fog lifted. I saw with sudden clarity that I didn't want
that future. Not with him.

I deleted his messages.

Bad men will pull you into their chaos and call it intimacy. They'll make surviving them feel like proof that you love them.
But the ones who refuse to face their own pain?
They'll bleed it all over your life and call it passion.

I learned to stop romanticizing the storm.

I learned something else, too. Something crucial.

That loneliness is temporary. Regret from settling isn't.

That the right person won't require assembly.

...

My dating life was never the struggle that women's magazines insisted it should be. Men fell in love with me easily. Too easily, sometimes.

The art gallery owner who asked me to move in after our third date.
The startup CEO who wrote me terrible poetry, before we'd even slept together. (Not that it would've been a good time for it then...or ever.)
The architect who planned our hypothetical wedding after two weeks.

I wasn't playing games. I wasn't strategic. I just showed up as myself: opinionated, curious, unfiltered. This drove certain men wild.

"You're not like other women," they'd say, as if that were the ultimate praise. As if being grouped with other women was somehow insulting. Which revealed everything about them and nothing about me.

Men who hate women, but make an exception for you, aren't offering a compliment. They're confessing.

What they meant was: You're not performing. You're not trying to be whatever you think I want. You're just... yourself.

It was strange. Being myself, the thing I'd been told would drive men away, was precisely what drew them in.

But here was the catch: while they were falling head over heels, I was usually underwhelmed. I'd listen to their declarations, watch their eager eyes searching my face for equal enthusiasm, and feel that familiar sinking feeling.

Because for all their passion, most of them didn't want *me*. They wanted the idea of me. The challenge. The woman who didn't immediately bend to their will or mirror their desires. They wanted to be the one who "won" me.

And once they thought they had? That's when the requests would start. Small at first.

"Maybe don't be so direct in front of my friends."
"Could you just let me finish my thought before questioning it?"
"Do you have to have an opinion on everything?"

They fell in love with the storm, then tried to tame it. Admired my fire, then asked me to dim it. They wanted the thrill of a woman who stood her ground, until that ground opposed theirs.

The pattern revealed itself with perfect clarity: Dating was easy. Finding someone who truly wanted me to remain myself? That was the challenge.

Those false starts weren't failures. They were necessary reconnaissance. Each man who loved the idea of me, but not the reality, helped clarify exactly what I wouldn't compromise. Each relationship that fizzled when I refused to collapse into a version they could manage taught me something. Being "worse," more myself, less accommodating wasn't just acceptable. It was essential.

It turns out that being easily desired isn't the same as being truly seen. And I'd rather be truly seen by one person than superficially desired by a hundred.

But getting there required unlearning years of conditioning. My friends would analyze texts for hidden meanings, rehearse what to say, strategize their every move. Always asking, *Does he like me? Am I doing this right?*

I did the same thing. We all did.

Our focus stayed so fixed on being chosen that we rarely paused to ask if we actually wanted to choose him back.

I'd listen to friends describe mediocre dates with men who barely asked them questions, men who talked over them, men who couldn't be bothered to remember the simplest details about their lives, and still, they'd hope for a call back.

It wasn't because we lacked worth or wisdom. It was something more insidious. The slow drip of messages we'd all absorbed since girlhood that twisted the wiring in our brains until being wanted was more important than wanting. That the goal wasn't mutual desire, but simply being desired.

I fell into this trap too, sometimes. But something stubborn in me always woke up and whispered, *But do YOU like HIM?* And too often, the answer was no.

...

I once flew to New York City for a romantic weekend and bailed in under 24 hours. The kind of escape that requires calling airlines and explaining to customer service representatives why you need to flee a city like it's on fire.

It happened during that strange limbo after becoming single again, when you're simultaneously relieved and terrified by your own freedom. I'd reconnected with a suitor from my past, someone I met in New York years earlier, on one of those nights when everyone seems more interesting than they actually are. A charming maybe who lingered in the background of my dating history like a missed flight, always wondering "what if" but never worth rebooking.

I had a clear memory from our past: dinner where his gorgeous ex-girlfriend made a surprise appearance. Beauty pageant gorgeous. The kind of gorgeous that makes you hyperaware of your own pores.

If he could pull someone like that, maybe I'd underestimated him?

He invited me to watch the World Cup with him for the weekend. Casual. Low-pressure. Just two adults enjoying international soccer and each other's company.

Flirty conversation, nothing serious. The kind of banter that feels harmless over the phone.

By the time I got home that day, his secretary had emailed me an itinerary. I was leaving the next morning.

Apparently, my flirting skills are...potent.

Everything happened too quickly for me to consider the implications of spending an entire weekend with someone. Would we share a bed? Would he expect something I wasn't ready to give? Did I even *like* him enough for any of this?

Questions I absolutely should have asked before packing my bag and boarding a plane.

He took me to a nice dinner after I arrived. I chose to overlook the fact that he was wearing a *cuff bracelet* and had his shirt unbuttoned one button too low. A detail that should have been my first warning.

Warning signs don't always scream. Sometimes they whisper. Sometimes they wear cuff bracelets.

Back at his place, both tired from the day, we decided to sleep. He didn't ask if I was comfortable sharing a bed. Just assumed we would. That assumption should have been my cue to call a cab. Instead, I went to the bathroom to change and when I emerged in a tank top and sweats, he was already sprawled across the bed covered by what I can only describe as a napkin masquerading as a blanket.

He was topless. I couldn't tell if he was wearing anything beneath the napkin-blanket. I had no desire to investigate.

I climbed into bed, positioning myself as far to the opposite side as physics would allow. The air conditioner blasted at what felt like subzero temperatures, forcing me closer to the napkin-blanket I'd been avoiding. I curled into a ball, turned away from him, clutching the corner of that pathetic excuse for coverage and my last shred of peace.

At some point, I fell asleep. Only to be jolted awake by his arm draped across me.
Dead weight.
The kind that feels deliberate in its pretense of accidental placement.

His hands wandered.
I perfected the art of fake sleep.
Inched closer and closer to the edge of the bed until gravity became my second concern.

All that kept running through my mind: *Three. More. Nights.*

THREE MORE NIGHTS of fighting him off.

The next morning he woke me at a criminally early hour and started blaring techno.
Not gentle morning jazz.
Not soft acoustic melodies.
Aggressive, pulsing techno.

I don't like waking up to find myself in the middle of Neon Carnival without warning. Or drugs.

I buried myself under the pillow. Disappeared, or tried to.

"Wake up!" he shouted.

"I'm tired. Need more sleep," I mumbled.

"But it's 9!"

"NOT in San Diego. In San Diego, it's 6! Turn this music off, it's giving me a headache."

He considered this momentarily. "Okay, I'll put on some Enya."

And he did.

With sleep clearly out of the question, I surrendered to consciousness. I retreated to the shower, where I took deep calming breaths that did absolutely nothing to calm me.

I got dressed while he showered.

And then I packed my bag.

By the time he emerged from the bathroom, I was fully dressed, zipped, and ready to go.

I left.

No explanation. I was young and uncomfortable and just wanted to escape: from him, from the napkin-blanket, from the techno-turned-Enya, from all of it.

I called my brother to discuss my travel options.

"I need a ticket home."

"How much is a ticket?" he asked, practical as always.

"I have no idea."

"If it's a lot, just stay there and have sex with him."

Brotherly wisdom at its finest.

I called the airline and discovered every flight to San Diego was sold out for two days. I explained my situation to the woman on the phone in excruciating detail. Told her about the techno, and the napkin-blanket. About how he kept his shirt unbuttoned so low it was practically a cardigan. How his hands had "accidentally" wandered during the night like confused tourists. How he'd replaced normal morning conversation with Enya at concert volume.

"He played 'Orinoco Flow,' ma'am. At six in the morning. The *'sail away'* part...over and over. And then asked if I wanted pancakes. I felt spiritually trafficked."

There was a long pause on the line before she said, flatly, "This is an emergency," and proceeded to find me a flight to LA that evening.

It cost me five dollars.

A sliver of my dignity.
And the last of my naïveté.

When I stepped into the LAX arrivals area, exhausted
and just wanting to disappear, I spotted my brother.
And next to him...my dad.

My stomach dropped. I froze mid-step.

I had intentionally *not* called my father because...how
exactly do you explain to your dad that you fled a man's
apartment after one night? That you were running away
from unwanted touches and aggressive New Age
soundscaping?

Some things daughters prefer their fathers never know.

I was mortified. Heat rushed to my face as I approached
them, trying to compose an explanation that wouldn't
sound as pathetic as I felt.

My dad just smiled. Didn't ask for details I wasn't ready
to give. Just hugged me and helped with my bag, while
my brother made fun of me the entire drive home.

Looking back, it's one of my favorite memories. The
way my father showed up without judgment. The quiet
understanding in his eyes. The knowledge that no
matter what mess I found myself in, he'd be there at the
airport, standing beside my mocking brother, ready to
bring me home.

A beautiful moment. At my complete expense.

I didn't have language for it yet, but my body knew.
Something wasn't right, and I listened.

I chose the discomfort of an awkward exit over the prolonged discomfort of staying somewhere that felt wrong.
I chose to be worse at being polite.
And better at not betraying myself.

That version of me, young, uncertain, still learning, already understood something fundamental that would take me years to fully articulate.

Sometimes being difficult isn't difficult at all. Sometimes it's the path of least resistance between you and your own peace.

I still can't listen to Enya.

All I wanted was sleep. What I got was a spiritual hostage situation soundtracked by Celtic fusion.

This story, by the way, is my brother's favorite to tell at family gatherings. Nothing like your embarrassment becoming someone else's cherished anecdote.

I'll take the techno and the napkin-blanket as a reminder of what my body always knew.

That worse isn't always worse.
Sometimes it's just real.

...

My exit strategies evolved with practice. After the New York incident, there was the beach date disaster.

This one said he was "passionate about deep conversation." What he actually meant was listing random facts while I imagined my own death in vivid detail. After about an hour, I made it clear I was ready to leave.

"At least let me buy you dinner before you go," he said, like this was a reasonable compromise for wasting my evening.

We got takeout and he suggested eating it on the beach where we'd just walked. He assured me I could leave once I finished eating. Society's rules said this was reasonable: he bought food, I owed him time. The "good girl" would stay and eat.

So I sat on his blanket, taking microscopic bites of my food while mentally calculating how long was socially acceptable before I could claim fullness. Meanwhile, I stealthily tossed pieces of my meal off to the side, building a small shrine of discarded food in the darkness beyond the blanket.

"I'm done," I declared after seven minutes of performative chewing.

When we stood to leave, his flashlight beam caught my sad little pile of rejected food.

"Is...is that your dinner?" he asked, genuinely confused.

"I believe it's technically called an escape route," I replied, already walking toward my car.

I'd followed society's rules instead of my instincts and ended up creating a bizarre crime scene of discarded take-out. Politeness will kill you if you let it. The kind of death you walk into smiling.

...

Not every disappointment came wrapped in awkward silence and takeout.

Some of them texted good morning and brought coffee with unfailing consistency.

He was sweet. Cute. Attentive in all the surface ways. He'd bring me little gifts, ask how I slept.

On paper, perfect.

But something was missing. That spark of intellectual connection. The way conversations should unfold like endless staircases, each thought leading to another, higher, more interesting one. With him, conversations felt like perfectly pleasant circles. Round and round we'd go, never quite breaking new ground.

I tried to end things gently. He begged for another chance.

"Just tell me what's wrong," he said, desperate and earnest. "I can fix it."

How do you tell someone that what's missing isn't something they can fix? That you don't find them intellectually stimulating enough to build a future with? That their mind doesn't challenge yours in ways that make you want to stay?

I fumbled through the usual soft exits. "Chemistry." "Different wavelengths." "Not quite clicking."

He saw through each one, his frustration growing.

Finally, truth slipped out. "I just don't think we connect intellectually in the way I need."

His face flushed. First hurt, then indignation. As if I'd slapped him with words.

"What did the last guy you dated do for a living?" he demanded. As if profession was the perfect proxy for intellect. As if degrees and job titles could measure the thing I found missing between us.

I hesitated. Not because I couldn't remember, but because I knew the answer would only wound him more.

"He was a neurosurgeon."

The silence that followed would have been tragic if it wasn't so unintentionally comic. The universe's punchline to a joke I never meant to tell.

Later, at home, I laughed until I cried. Not at him, but at the ridiculous theater of it all. At how we try to quantify connection. At how we search for concrete reasons when the truth is so much simpler: some minds just don't dance well together.

I wondered if there was a kinder way I could have ended things. But maybe honesty, even when it stings, is its own form of kindness.

...

There was the judge. At his house. A second date that never really began.

His modern house with glass and steel and opinions about architecture.

He'd left it on the perfect white couch like some bizarre centerpiece. Oversized. Staring with glassy eyes that reflected nothing back. The kind of gift you'd give a child or a girlfriend of three months in high school.

I stared at it. Wondering what message he thought this conveyed. What version of me existed in his mind that would clutch this monstrosity to her chest and squeal with delight.

The script was clear. My role was to overflow with gratitude. To perform the feminine surprise and joy women are taught to express regardless of how they actually feel...

I couldn't do it.

"It's a stuffed animal," I said flatly. "I'm thirty-four."

The silence stretched between us like taffy pulling thinner and thinner.

His face tightened with offense. As if my honest response was the transgression, not his bizarre gift. As if the script demanded my delight, not my authenticity.

What bothered me wasn't just the bear with its vacant stare. It was what it revealed. That he saw me as something simple. Something to be placated with childish tokens. That beneath the polished exterior of a man who shaped verdicts and directed court proceedings was someone who didn't understand that grown women don't hoard stuffed animals like emotional support items.

The evening imploded from there. My honesty hanging between us like broken glass, impossible to step around. Every attempt at conversation afterward felt like trudging through quicksand. His resentment palpable. My refusal to apologize for my truth even more so.

I never saw him again. Sometimes I wonder if that bear still sits on his pristine couch. Waiting for a woman who knows how to perform the expected delight. One who understands that in the dating world, a woman's authentic response is often less valued than her ability to make a man feel good about his choices, no matter how misguided.

He wanted the cute expression of overwhelmed gratitude. The performance of girlish joy.

I wanted jewelry. Or books. Or nothing at all.

Like adults.

...

The dating stories? Those are easy. Light. Funny. Occasionally absurd.

But not all of them were.

He met my dad.

After my dad died, the idea of starting over with someone who'd never known him felt unbearable.

Maybe that's why I stayed. Longer than I should have.

He was the last boyfriend who ever met my dad.
Walking away felt like losing my father all over again.

Which is how I ended up heartbroken over a former
model with the emotional range of a countertop.

A man who once said he was tired of being "just a pretty
face and a big dick."

He announced it like it was a burden. Like we should
feel bad for him.

He was a snob. Not in the fun, self-aware way I am. In
that greasy, performative superiority way that makes
everyone else feel small so he could feel big.

And still, I stayed.
It is truly incredible what you cannot see, when you
cannot bear to see it.

I wasn't reckless. I was hopeful.
(Which is practically the same thing.)

But I got hurt anyway.

When that trust cracked, it felt like free-falling.
No ground.
No grip.
Just that panicked, breathless drop where all you're left
with are the questions: *Was it me? Did I miss the signs? Was
I not enough?*

The answer was simpler. While I was mourning my
father, he was fucking other women.

The friends I thought would catch me didn't. I withdrew
into myself, and they didn't even notice. Or worse, they

noticed and decided not to follow. I still don't know what cut deeper.

Loneliness comes in many forms. But the loneliness that follows betrayal is a particular kind of suffocation. The feeling of screaming underwater, of making noise that never reaches the surface.

It took months. Then years.
Just to find my footing.
To look at the wreckage and finally say: *That wasn't about me.*

I had loved honestly.
Completely.
Willingly.

But there's a cost to telling the truth, even to yourself. Once you admit what you tolerated, what you excused, what you begged to be enough, you can't unknow it. You can't pretend you didn't contort. That you didn't lower the bar and call it generosity. That you weren't secretly hoping he'd rise to meet a version of himself he never agreed to be. (He didn't. He was too busy lamenting the burden of being hot and well-hung.)

Sometimes the wrong reasons keep you in the right place to learn what you're actually worth.

...

I chased distraction so hard, I forgot what I was running from. That's how this one started.

His big ideas revealed themselves before I recognized the emptiness behind them. Grandiose theories costumed as substance. Intoxicating but ultimately hollow. I was running from grief, and he was running toward the next horizon. For a while, our escapes aligned.

The way he moved through life with such certainty. His stories, his adventures, his passion were captivating. It wasn't just about the experiences he shared; it was the intensity of his beliefs, the way he saw the world, and how deeply he felt everything.

It was easy to get lost in that. To imagine I could fit into his world, that I could belong there.

But in that space, I never truly found mine.

I kept quiet about the things I needed. Those little pieces of myself I was too afraid to express. The words I wanted to say, the parts of myself I wanted him to see stayed locked away. I told myself it didn't matter, that it was enough, that things would work themselves out.

But silence only grew louder with time.

Those unsaid words became harder to ignore. I carried them like stones in my pockets, weighing me down, knowing deep down that if I spoke them, it might change everything. Or worse, that he might not be able to give me what I needed in return.

I never told him how much I longed to be seen for who I truly was. Not just a part of his world, but as someone individually valued. How much I needed the kind of security that could only come from vulnerability and trust. That if I opened up, I needed to know that the space I made would be met with understanding, not just silence.

We never fought. We never raised our voices. But we also never fully let each other in.

And in that quiet, that space between us, I realized that we were never going to bridge that gap. It wasn't for lack of trying, but because we were standing on different sides, both unsure if we could cross over.

The silence became my answer.

But even now, those unsaid words stay with me. They're not regrets, but reminders of something we could never fully reach. A piece of what could have been.

And perhaps that's how it was meant to be: sometimes, silence holds more than words ever could.

...

I've talked about the worst ones. But not the hardest to let go.
Not every heartbreak is loud. One of mine was quiet. Almost right.

My favorite ex. Funny, confident, and charming. The kind of man who knows the power of eye contact and a subtle smirk. A total player. But the kind you willingly get played by. He had blue eyes like the man I'd eventually marry. Maybe that's why I looked too long. Maybe that's why I stayed a little too open.

We had fun. The kind that makes time stretch and blur. But he was in transition, sorting out his life while I was trying to build mine. He wasn't sure he wanted kids. I was sure I did. He moved back to the Midwest.

We stayed in touch longer than we should have.
Usually him. Late-night texts.
Check-ins that felt too intimate for people no longer together.
I didn't always answer.
But I didn't shut the door either.

He taught me that chemistry isn't the same as alignment. You can love someone's laugh and their mind and still know your futures don't speak the same language.

He was lovely.
Just not mine.

...

These ghosts were with me that day in the coffee shop, when KB slid into the chair beside me. Those histories whispered caution while I laughed too easily, talked too freely, felt too much too soon.

Each heartbreak was research. Each almost-right person, data collection.

The alcoholic taught me that saving someone isn't love; it's just another form of control.

The one who betrayed me taught me trust isn't naive; it's necessary.

The worldly one taught me distraction isn't intimacy.

The rebound taught me kindness without connection isn't sustainable; some minds simply don't dance well together.

The New York escape taught me to trust my instincts; my body already knew what my mind was still processing.

And as KB and I talked for hours that first day, something quiet settled in me. A recognition. Not fireworks. Not destiny. Just a simple *oh, there you are.*

It terrified me.

By then, I knew love wasn't safe.
Letting someone in meant handing them a loaded gun and hoping they wouldn't use it.
Vulnerability was just another word for future pain.

I'd built careful walls. Brick by brick. Heartbreak by heartbreak. I'd constructed a fortress around the softest parts of myself, and I decorated it beautifully so no one would notice it was a fortress at all.

Then KB walked in and didn't even notice the walls. Just stepped right through them like they weren't there.

Six weeks later, we moved in together.

My friends thought I was crazy. My mother was sure it would end in disaster. My brother asked if I was pregnant.

For once in my life, I wasn't overthinking. I wasn't playing it safe. I wasn't trying to be "better" or more subdued or easier to love. I was just...following what felt right. Being fully myself, with all my sharp edges and loud opinions and inconvenient truths.

For once in my life, I was choosing love without armor.

...

No one prepared me for meeting "the one."

It was calm and charged, steady and electric.

You don't feel ready. You just feel ruined in a new way.

Something cracked open in me I hadn't realized was sealed.

And then time stopped behaving. Four hours felt like minutes. And somehow, also, like we'd known each other forever.

I used to laugh at love stories that claimed "when you know, you know." It seemed so ridiculous. So naive.

But then I knew.

...

KB is easygoing in a way I'm not. He moves through the world with this quiet grace. Steady. Reliable. The kind of calm that absorbs my wildness.

Not perfect. Never that. Just present.

There are moments when I catch him watching me. Not the polished version. Not the version I think the world wants to see. But me. Raw. Unfiltered. Unguarded.

Love isn't about smoothing edges. It's about seeing them. Tracing their sharp lines. Understanding that complexity isn't a flaw.

Sometimes I wonder how we work. How two people can create something so...whole.

He listens. Not just to my words. But to the spaces between them. To the silence that holds more truth than anything I could say.

When the world tries to flatten me. Reduce me to something manageable. Predictable. He expands. Makes more room. Refuses to let me be anything less than exactly who I am.

Sometimes I think about this. How strange it is to feel so secure in something. To know with absolute certainty that the foundation won't crack. No matter how much weight you put on it. (And I'm not known for being gentle with things.)

It's a different kind of miracle. Less dramatic than my usual chaos. No less profound.

Quiet.
Steady.
Certain.

I'm the earthquake. He's the ground that doesn't break.

In a world where my intensity was always too much, his stability became the only place I never had to apologize for shaking things up.

...

When KB and I eloped, I wore a simple white dress that had been hanging in my closet for years, unworn, as if waiting for precisely this moment. No elaborate ceremony. No months of planning. Just us, promising each other forever in front of a justice of the peace, exactly one year after that coffee shop meeting.

"I don't believe in marriage," he'd told me that very first day. "And I never want kids."

"Then I'll never date you," I'd replied, certain.

Yet there we were. Making liars of ourselves in the most beautiful way.

After the ceremony, we returned to the coffee shop where we'd met, then had dinner at the restaurant where we had our first date. A perfect circle. Uncomplicated. True.

Like everything with KB.

...

I'm sure other women had different experiences with KB. Women who dated him before me. Who thought they knew him.
But this is my book. Not theirs.
I could've included their perspectives for a more well-rounded picture, but they all declined to comment. (Hard to decline when you're never actually asked, but semantics.)

They skipped our wedding. Didn't even RSVP. Didn't even send a gift.

Which felt rude, considering I'd already mentally seated them at table six.

We had similar taste in men. I figured we'd have plenty to talk about.

Shared stories. A few laughs. Compare notes.

I thought we'd become friends.

Maybe they'd understand why he couldn't commit to them.

And why he couldn't *not* commit to me.

I wanted them to like me more than they ever liked him. Preferably while spilling all his secrets.

I wanted them to see what he saw.

To understand why it was different with me.

Why he stayed.

Why he bought a ring.

Why he planned a future.

Not because I changed him.

But because I was his exact type of chaos.

I wanted them to walk away thinking,

Yeah, I get it.

I would've chosen her too.

Is that delusional? Probably.

I genuinely thought we could be friends.

Bonded over our shared experience of loving the same impossible man. Except with me, he loved back differently.

The ex-girlfriend alliance probably meets for drinks sometimes. Same bar, same story. Discussing the one who got away, except he didn't get away. He just found someone who made staying more interesting than running.

Probably easier to believe he changed.
Maybe that's the cleaner story.
Clean stories don't sting as much.
But they don't stick either.
The alternative cuts deeper.
He was always capable of commitment.
Just not with them.

...

I look at KB sometimes, across the dinner table or in the early morning light, and I'm grateful he loves my kind of worse. The kind of worse that doesn't filter thoughts for palatability. The kind of worse that takes up space without constantly checking if it's inconveniencing someone.

The kind of worse that won't trade edge for affection.

Before KB, I thought love meant performance. I thought it meant being better. Better at compromise (which usually meant surrender), better at patience (which usually meant silence), better at understanding (which usually meant accepting the unacceptable).

I am the kind of worse that refuses to negotiate my basic worth. The kind of worse that won't apologize for having standards. The kind of worse that recognizes my time as valuable and doesn't waste it on people who don't deserve it.

The kind of worse that held out for what I deserved, even when it meant being alone longer than others thought I should be.

I wonder if he knows. If he understands that he saved me not by fixing me or changing me, but by loving me exactly as I am.

By showing me that I didn't have to be "better" to be worthy of love.

That I could be messy and difficult and completely myself, and still be someone's forever.

That love isn't about finding your missing piece or your better half, but about finding someone who makes you want to be your whole self.

Someone who looks at all your wild parts and doesn't try to tame them.

Someone who sees you.

Who builds a life with you not despite your complexities, but because of them.

I look at him, and I think: *This. This is what they should tell little girls about love.*

Not fairy tales. Not rescues. Not happily ever afters.

But this. The real, unfiltered truth of what it means to love and be loved without conditions or expectations.

The truth that love is an unpredictable path.
Sometimes beautiful.
Sometimes brutal.

Always worth it.

If only I'd known sooner that I didn't need to trade pieces of myself just to be chosen.

That the right kind of love would give me room to grow.

That being "worse," less accommodating, more authentic, fiercely true to myself wouldn't push love away.

It would finally, *finally* let it in.

the c word

Three doctors told me I was depressed. Turns out I was dying.

My body knew first. Before the doctors with their practiced sympathy. Before the word malignant crashed into my life like an uninvited guest who refuses to leave.

I knew something wasn't right.
A heaviness. A fatigue too profound to be normal.
Like someone had turned down the volume on my life and expected me not to notice.
My body felt like it was moving through mud.

I went to doctors, again and again. Each time, they insisted I was depressed. Just stressed. Just tired. Just a woman who needed to stop being so dramatic about her own mortality.

"Take these," they said, pushing prescriptions for antidepressants across their desks, avoiding my eyes. "You'll feel better."

I never filled them. Something deep down whispered *this isn't depression.*

What I didn't know was that it was cancer. The same monster that had taken my father was now growing inside me, quiet and patient, waiting to be discovered.

...

The timing felt like cosmic cruelty.

KB and I were newlyweds from our elopement, ink barely dry on those papers. We were planning our wedding ceremony, dreaming of dancing and celebrating with everyone we loved (and 100 of my mom's guests we couldn't pick out of a lineup). Promising forever to each other all over again, this time surrounded by witnesses.

Cancer has a way of redefining forever. Of collapsing time until all that exists is the present moment, the next breath, the next heartbeat.

The day of my diagnosis remains a blur, which is probably mercy disguised as trauma response. Some moments are too large for memory to hold properly.

I remember fragments: the fluorescent lights of the doctor's office humming like dying insects, casting that particular shade of institutional green that makes everyone look like they're already deceased. The plastic chairs that squeaked every time KB shifted his weight.

The diplomas on the wall that suddenly seemed less impressive and more like decorative props in a very expensive theater of doom.

KB's hand was warm and steady in mine while my world tilted sideways, his fingers interlocked with mine like he could anchor me to reality through sheer force of will. The doctor's careful voice saying "malignant" and "surgical options" with the practiced neutrality of someone who delivers apocalypses for a living.

Something about stages and margins and protocols. Something about choices that never felt like choices at all.

The word malignant hung in the air like fine dust. I watched it settle over everything, the medical journals, the family photos on his desk, the motivational poster about perseverance that now felt like dark comedy.

I nodded as if we were discussing someone else's body. Someone else's future. Someone else's suddenly uncertain expiration date. As if this conversation was happening to a character in a movie I was watching.

The strange calm in my voice as I asked practical questions: treatment plans, recovery time, success rates, while something fundamental inside me shattered into pieces so small I'm still finding them years later.

Then the silent car ride home.

That's what no one tells you about receiving life-altering news: how ruthlessly unchanged everything looks afterward. The same streets you've driven a thousand times. The same traffic lights stopping the same cars filled with people whose biggest worry is what to make for dinner. The same world continuing its relentless spin as if nothing had changed.

While your entire existence has been cleaved into before and after.

Again.

Before, when cancer was something that happened to other people.

After, when you realize you *are* other people.

KB drove with the careful attention of someone transporting something fragile. Which, I suppose, he was. Neither of us spoke. What do you say when a doctor has just rewritten your life story in medical terminology? The radio played some cheerful pop song about summer love, completely tone-deaf to the gravity of our situation.

I stared out the window and watched people living their normal Tuesday, completely unaware that in the car passing them on the right, someone was learning how to exist in a body that had just been reclassified as potentially temporary.

The cancer diagnosis came like a thunderclap in a clear sky. Unexpected. World-shattering. The kind of plot twist that makes you question every moment of happiness that came before it, wondering if they were just setting you up for this particular fall.

When we got home, I stood in our bathroom, staring at myself in the mirror. Still looking like me. Still feeling like me, mostly. Wondering how something so deadly could be growing inside without any external evidence. My body, both mine, and suddenly a stranger's.

I cried that night. Not delicate tears sliding gracefully down cheeks, but the ugly guttural sobs of someone mourning a future suddenly uncertain. KB held me, his chest against my back, his arms a fortress around my trembling body. The taste of salt on my lips. The sound of my own heartbeat thundering in my ears as if to remind me I was still alive, still here, despite the cells rebelling inside me.

"I'm sorry," I kept repeating, though I couldn't articulate for what exactly. For bringing this into our new marriage. For the possibility of leaving sooner than promised. For the wedding we might not have. For everything. The guilt was irrational, but overwhelming. As if I had somehow tricked him, offered him a whole woman only to reveal I might be broken. As if I had failed at being a wife before we'd even had our wedding ceremony.

"Don't" he whispered fiercely. "Don't apologize for something that isn't your fault."

This fear had been with me since that day in the doctor's office. I watched KB's face as the doctor spoke. Searched for regret. For the thought I knew must be crossing his mind: *This isn't what I signed up for.*

Instead, I saw something else. A quiet determination. A love that suddenly had edges, teeth.

"We've got this," he said. Not *you've* got this. *We've.*

And just like that, my body wasn't just mine anymore. It was ours. This battlefield, this sacred ground, this temporary home whose lease might be ending sooner than we'd planned.

...

"I won't blame you if you want out," I told KB one night, after the diagnosis but before surgery, when the weight of uncertainty felt heavier than I could bear. I couldn't even look at him as I said it. "You didn't sign up for this."

He was quiet for so long that I thought maybe he was actually considering it. My heart shattered in the silence.

Then he sat down beside me, took my hand in his, and said, "I didn't sign up for cancer. I signed up for you. For us. For whatever comes with that."

In that moment, I understood something about love that none of my previous relationships had taught me: Real love isn't about the fantasy. It's not about the perfect moments or the romantic gestures or the happily-ever-afters.

Real love is about showing up. It's about holding space for pain. It's about staying when it would be easier to run.

I thought of the alcoholic. How easy it had been to delete his messages. How impossible it would be to delete KB from my heart.

The difference was in me. In who I'd become. In what I'd learned to recognize as love.

...

The surgery date loomed. A red circle on a calendar that seemed to bleed into every day that came before it.

The decision to postpone surgery, to walk down the aisle without a scar, wasn't just vanity...though that's what I told myself at the time. It was defiance. A refusal to let cancer dictate every aspect of my life. A need to create one perfect day where I could pretend everything was normal. Where I could dance and laugh and promise forever without the shadow of my mortality hanging over us.

There's something so primal about wanting to protect moments of pure joy from the shadow of illness. To create one untouched space where cancer doesn't get to intrude. One perfect day where I could be just a bride, not a patient. One collection of photographs where I was whole, unmarked, still carrying all original parts of myself.

I became an expert in compartmentalization. Wedding planning in the morning. Medical research in the afternoon. Trying on dresses one day, discussing survival rates the next. Looking at flower arrangements while mentally preparing for what my body would be like after surgery. In one email thread, I confirmed the wedding DJ; in another, I scheduled pre-operative appointments. The cognitive dissonance was exhausting and surreal, planning for the beginning of a marriage and the possibility of its premature end.

The strangest part wasn't the cancer itself. It was living in two realities simultaneously.

Tuesday morning: researching survival rates and surgical options, taking notes in a spiral notebook like I was studying for the world's most fucked up final exam.

Tuesday afternoon: tasting wedding cakes with my mother, nodding enthusiastically about buttercream versus fondant while mentally calculating recovery time. "The lemon is divine," the baker said, watching me take another bite.

I smiled and agreed, thinking: Will I be able to eat solid food by the reception?

Wednesday: calling the florist to discuss centerpieces.

Thursday: calling the surgeon to discuss margins.

The conversations blurred together. Peonies and pathology reports. Seating charts and surgical schedules. My brain compartmentalized with terrifying efficiency, as if planning a wedding while dying was just another Tuesday.

KB found me one night, surrounded by bridal magazines and medical printouts, cross-referencing dates like I was solving a puzzle instead of planning around my own mortality.

"This is insane," he said quietly.

"Which part?" I asked. "The cancer or the centerpieces?"

"Both. Neither. I don't know."

Neither did I. But somehow, planning the perfect day felt like insurance against not having any days left. As if the universe wouldn't dare interrupt such careful coordination.

I smiled in our engagement photos with a secret lodged in my chest. I tasted wedding cakes and chose flowers and picked out my dress while part of me was already grieving. I danced at our reception with scans and surgical dates buzzing in the back of my mind like persistent insects.

I lived in that liminal space between joy and fear. Between celebration and mourning. Between the woman I had been and the one I was about to become.

Our wedding video shows me laughing, radiant, seemingly carefree. What it doesn't show is how tightly I gripped KB's hand under the table during dinner. How I excused myself once to cry in the bathroom, overwhelmed by the weight of what was coming. How I memorized every moment with a desperate intensity, knowing that after this day, everything would change.

How do you tell someone you've known for just over a year that they might have signed up for a much shorter "forever" than either of you planned?

I didn't cry when they marked my body with purple pen, drawing maps for the surgeon to follow. I didn't cry when I signed consent forms that listed death as a possible side effect. I didn't cry when they wheeled me away from KB, his face growing smaller as they pushed me down a hallway that felt endless.

I cried later. When I woke up with part of me removed. When I looked in the mirror and saw the incision. Terrain I didn't recognize. A landscape carved by survival.

The pain wasn't what I expected. Not sharp or stabbing like in movies. It was deep. Cellular. The kind of hurt that feels ancient, like your body remembering every injury it's ever sustained all at once.

And in those first days of recovery, a thought that terrified me more than cancer ever had: What if I couldn't have children now?

I didn't know yet that finding out would take four years and cost me in ways I couldn't predict.

...

The fertility doctors spoke in percentages. They measured my hope in follicle counts and hormone levels. My future, reduced to graphs and charts that looked like the stock market during a recession.

"Your body has been through trauma," one doctor said, her voice gentle but clinical. "We need to be realistic about expectations."

Realistic.
As if nearly dying hadn't already recalibrated my sense of realistic.

I was already injecting myself with hormones that turned me into a bloated rage monster. How much more realistic did she want me to get?

As if I hadn't endured countless internal ultrasounds, my dignity left at the door along with my clothes. As if KB and I hadn't transformed our bedroom into a medical supply station, our nightstands cluttered with alcohol swabs and sharps containers instead of lube and sex toys. The things that make sex about pleasure instead of procreation.

After our first IVF cycle, when we only got one embryo, KB couldn't hide his frustration. One chance. Just one. He wanted more. I wanted to give him more. I wondered if beneath it all, he was disappointed in me. In what my body couldn't do.

We tried again. And again. Four failed cycles, each one its own private funeral.

We didn't name them, these potential children who never materialized. But I felt them like ghosts. Possibilities that haunted empty rooms in our house.

...

The miscarriage brought a sorrow I wasn't prepared for.

Loss registers differently in different bodies. In mine, it carved out a hollow space. A physical emptiness that matched the emotional void.

For twelve weeks, I let myself believe.

Twelve weeks where I stopped bracing for loss. Where I let my guard down just enough to imagine. A nursery. A name. The weight of a baby in my arms.

We'd seen a heartbeat on a monitor at 8 weeks. That flickering rhythm on a grainy screen that looked like static but meant everything. We'd heard the whoosh-whoosh-whoosh that proved something alive was growing inside me. Something that had beaten the odds. Something that made it past the first trimester danger zone everyone warns you about.

I'd started to relax. Started to believe my body could actually do this.

The twelve week appointment was supposed to be routine. Hear the heartbeat again. Exhale. Start telling people beyond our inner circle.

I remember what I wore. Jeans I could still button. A loose shirt that hid nothing yet. That dangerous feeling of almost-safe.

My OB put the doppler on my belly.

Moved it.

Moved it again.

Her face changed before she said anything. That professional mask slipping for just a second. Long enough for me to know.

"Let me try the ultrasound," she said. Her voice too careful. Too gentle.

The screen that had shown that flickering heartbeat four weeks earlier showed nothing. A dark space where rhythm should have been. A body that had stopped growing. Had stopped developing. Had simply stopped.

My OB cried as she told me. Actually cried. She knew everything we'd been through to get here. Every failed cycle. Every loss. Every hope we'd poured into this pregnancy.

I didn't cry.

Not then.

I nodded. Asked practical questions. When would I miscarry naturally? Did I need a D&C? What were the risks? Could we try again?

As if any of those answers mattered.

As if anything mattered when the thing growing inside me had died and my body hadn't even noticed.

They sent me home to wait. To let my body catch up to what had already happened. To walk around carrying death inside me for days while we scheduled the procedure to remove what my body should have expelled on its own but didn't.

I made it to the car before I broke.

KB found me on the bathroom floor that night. I don't remember walking there. Don't remember how long I'd been sitting on the cold tile with my back against the bathtub.

He didn't try to move me. Didn't ask if I was okay. Didn't say anything would be okay.

He just sat beside me. His back against the bathtub. His shoulder touching mine.

We breathed together in that small room. In and out. The only sound between us.

"I don't know how to help you," he said finally. His voice breaking. "Tell me what you need."

What I needed was impossible.

I needed twelve weeks back. I needed to not know what hope felt like before it was ripped away. I needed my body to work. I needed a world without babies on every corner, without pregnancy announcements in my feed, without friends casually complaining about morning sickness like it was an inconvenience instead of a privilege.

I needed the ability to unhear that silence where a heartbeat used to be.

I needed to stop seeing that empty space on the ultrasound screen every time I closed my eyes.

Most of all, I needed someone to tell me why. Why my body had killed the one thing I wanted most. Why I'd been allowed to believe for twelve whole weeks. Why hope was given just to be taken away.

I reached for his hand.
A small gesture.

It's strange how private these pains are. How you can be shopping for groceries or sitting in traffic or laughing at a friend's joke while carrying this enormous absence inside you.

How the world expects you to function when you're shattered.

How you somehow do.

...

I believed my body had betrayed me.

Through surgery. Through scars that changed my landscape forever. Through wondering if KB could still find me beautiful like this. Broken like this.

Through failed IVF attempts. Through the monthly grief of periods that arrived like clockwork to remind me what my body couldn't do.

Through miscarriage. Through the particular, hollow ache of loving someone you'll never meet. Through the way people avoid your eyes. Through the silence where congratulations had so recently lived.

I believed my body was broken. That I was broken.

I thought fertility would be like everything else I'd tackled: difficult, but solvable. Research plus effort equals results. Basic math.

"It might take a few months," I told KB with a shrug. "But we'll get there."

Months turned into a year. Then, two. Each month brought evidence that hope had overstayed its welcome.

The language of infertility is inherently accusatory. Hostile uterus. Incompetent cervix. Failed implantation. Miscarriage. As if your body is deliberately sabotaging you. As if reproduction is a test you're simply too stupid to pass.

I accumulated diagnoses like badges of shame. Diminished ovarian reserve. Post-cancer complications. Each one another reason why my body couldn't perform this supposedly natural function.

For me, it was physical. Every failed cycle lived not just in my heart but in my cells. My body pumped full of hormones, invaded by ultrasound wands, bled out monthly like clockwork.

For KB, it was emotional but abstract. He felt the disappointment, shared the grief, carried the weight of our shared dream deferred. But his body remained unchanged. Unaltered. Uninvaded.

We were experiencing the same loss through different lenses, feeling the same pain in different ways.

Nothing helped. Not the statistics. Not his hand on my back in clinic bathrooms.

But even in that rhythm of loss, something unspoken was happening. My body kept trying. Despite me cursing it. Despite me doubting it.

...

My body survived cancer.

Not because I willed it to. Not because I was stronger or braver or more deserving than those who don't survive.

But because some combination of medical science, cellular luck, and stubborn resilience carried me through.

My body endured fertility treatments. Needles. Hormones. Monthly failures.

My body held life. Lost it. Held it again.

And eventually, my body created Grayson.

Not because I earned it. Not because I manifested it. Not because I did anything right.

Just because bodies are unpredictable. Mysterious. Wildly beyond control.

Some miracles come on their own timeline, or not at all.

...

The first time I nursed him, I wept.
Not gentle, cinematic tears. Not even the sobs I'd come to know so well. This was something stranger. A cry scraped from somewhere older than memory.

Grief.
Joy.
Terror.
All of it crashing at once.

KB thought something was wrong.

The nurse hovered, concerned.

But nothing was wrong.

My body was feeding him.
The same body I'd spent years cursing.

My body wasn't broken.
It was just mine.

Scarred, difficult, unreliable, and somehow still here.

...

I was done apologizing for my body.
Done hiding it.
Done letting others decide what it should or shouldn't do.

My body had carried me through cancer. Through grief.
Through fertility struggles and pregnancy and birth.

...

There's a certain language you only learn in the company of others who've danced at the edge of death.

Nobody warns you about making friends at cancer camp. A week in the wilderness spent doing an outdoor activity. We forged instant bonds over our shared experience of becoming medical guinea pigs with uncertain expiration dates, friends who disappeared when treatment got "too depressing," and the particular horror of realizing the world keeps spinning while yours stands completely still.

But the truly fucked up part? Nobody ever mentions that when you make friends at cancer camp, people start dropping dead rather quickly. It's like the world's most morbid game of musical chairs, except instead of losing your seat, you lose your heartbeat. That class reunion photo becomes a grotesque version of "Guess Who?" The question isn't "Does your person wear glasses?" It's "Is your person still breathing?" I spent the day with one of these friends recently, both of us laughing about this reality. Just two people who've had cancer comparing notes on who didn't make it. (And who we wish hadn't.)

Brutal honesty without filters becomes your native language when you've stared down mortality while everyone else was building careers and starting families. Cancer teaches you to build connections knowing they might be temporary, to value authentic moments over sanitized sentiments. To recognize that some bridges aren't meant to be burned because life might torch them for you anyway.

...

There's no ceremony for survival.
No medals. No closure. Just the after.

KB snapped a photo the night after surgery.
I looked like hell.
Which felt about right.
Also, I looked radioactive, which honestly felt earned.

No inspirational bullshit. No "fighter" captions. Just evidence.

Proof that I didn't die.

Proof that survival isn't a makeover montage.
It's a body you barely recognize, still breathing. Still here.
It wasn't resilience. It was spite.

Months later, he caught me staring at it.
"Why do you keep that?"

Because it's the only picture that ever told the truth.

I didn't survive to be pretty for anyone.
I survived to be worse.

Also, my breasts look phenomenal in it.

...

The night before that photo was taken, I'd already launched my campaign against medical politeness.

A nurse came in to check my vitals. She had that forced cheerfulness of someone who's seen too many bad outcomes to be genuinely optimistic.

"And how are we feeling tonight?" she chirped, somehow making "we" sound like she'd also had parts of her body removed that day.

"I don't know how *we're* feeling," I mumbled, groggy from pain meds. "But I feel like someone hollowed me out with an ice cream scoop."

She laughed nervously, clearly expecting the polite patient script: *I'm fine, just a little sore, thanks for asking.*

"On a scale of one to ten, how's your pain?" she continued, already reaching for the chart.

"It's somewhere between labor and being eaten alive by something with bad table manners."

She blinked. "I'm not sure how to chart that."

"Think medieval torture device with modern efficiency," KB said from his chair.

"So, an eight?" she tried.

"Write down that my pain level is 'existential with a side of physical trauma.' Let's see what the doctor makes of that."

She actually wrote it down. Word for word.

I saw the resident's face the next morning when he read the chart, that brief moment of *what the fuck* before his professional mask slipped back into place.

The look on his face was the only pain relief I got that night.

...

My body doesn't look the same.
Obviously.
You don't walk through hell and come out pretty.
You come out possessed.

It's been opened up. Sewn shut. Pushed past breaking.
Expected to recover quietly.

I didn't survive to be quiet.
I didn't survive to make anyone comfortable.

And that's why I put my scar on the cover of this book.

Let them look.
It's the least they can do.

If they're going to stare, let it be at the truth.

...

I didn't have a diagnosis. Just a reputation.

"Difficult patient" is what they call you right before it turns out you were right.

Advocating for myself wasn't overreacting. It was survival.

I've learned that being a "good" woman means hiding the scars. Concealing the evidence. Not making others uncomfortable with your survival or your grief.

But I've also learned that being "good" almost killed me.

Being "good" meant swallowing my intuition when doctors dismissed my concerns.

Being "good" meant prioritizing others' comfort over my own healing.

Being "good" meant apologizing for my body instead of celebrating its resilience.

When I chose to be "worse," I chose to live. To advocate fiercely for my health when doctors wouldn't listen. To give my body time to heal on its own terms, not someone else's timeline. To use my body however I damn well pleased, whether that meant breastfeeding in public or showing my scars or taking up space without apology.

Being worse means I trust my body now. The one that survived. The one that knew what those doctors didn't. This scarred, imperfect, stubborn thing that refused to quit.

...

Being diagnosed with cancer at thirty-five taught me something about being worse that no amount of therapy or self-reflection ever could: my body doesn't exist for other people's comfort.

After surgery, my mother bought me a beautiful necklace, thinking it would help me feel less self-conscious about my throat scar. It was a gesture of love, but I never wore it. Not because I didn't appreciate the thought, but because I refused to treat my scar as something that needed concealing. Nothing says "I'm living my best life" quite like a neck accessory that screams "PLEASE DON'T NOTICE I ALMOST DIED."

Women are expected to make our suffering palatable. To disappear the parts of ourselves that might remind others of their mortality or make them confront the reality that bodies break, heal imperfectly, and carry the marks of our journeys. We're supposed to be tragic but tasteful. Damaged but decorous.

If my survival made people confront their own mortality, that wasn't my problem to solve. I didn't survive cancer to become a walking PSA or inspirational meme. I wasn't a tote bag. I was a liability.

When a coworker asked about my medical leave in that hushed, too-careful tone people use when they're more interested in the performance of concern than the answer, I didn't soften it with reassurances.

"Cancer," I said flat. Watching them scramble to respond appropriately. The look on their face. Like they'd accidentally ordered *truth* when they meant to order *small talk.*

Cancer stripped away my patience for performing wellness or hiding evidence of my struggles. It wasn't about being defiant for its own sake. It was about the simple math of energy conservation. I had exactly enough energy to heal, to love KB, to rebuild. I had zero energy left to manage other people's feelings about my body.

I once showed up to a work event with my scar visible for the first time. Some mid-level guy, a few drinks past functional, leaned in with that familiar strain of rehearsed sympathy. "My sister-in-law had cancer too," he said, like we were trauma twins. "She never talks about it. Very private. Very brave."

The message was clear: real strength doesn't ask to be seen.

"Oh, I'm thinking of getting it tattooed," I said, running a finger across the scar. "Tiny flames. Or a zipper. Something to make sure people don't miss it."

He choked on his wine. Not metaphorically. Someone had to hit his back.

Later, I heard him say I had "an unusual sense of humor for someone who's been through something like that."

I survived wrong. Next time I'll consult him on the proper way to nearly die.

Being worse at hiding, worse at apologizing, worse at making others comfortable with my reality wasn't just emotionally liberating. It was physically necessary. Every ounce of energy spent on performance was energy stolen from healing.

And after cancer, I became very selective about what deserved my energy.

Other people's comfort with my body didn't make the cut.
If I was going to survive, I was going to do it visibly. Off-script.
With a scar, a sense of humor, and no interest in pretending to be grateful for what almost killed me.

...

I'm worse now. About all of it.

Worse at hiding.
Worse at apologizing.
Worse at pretending I don't know exactly what I'm worth.

I'm not trying to be palatable.
I'm not interested in permission.

I'm the kind of worse that makes people nervous because I'm not performing discomfort for their comfort.

My body doesn't need a story that makes anyone else feel better.

I'm still here.
Scarred, difficult, breathing.

That's the whole plot.

the call is coming from inside the house

Some betrayals hit harder because they don't come from enemies. They come from friends. From people who were supposed to know better. People who once held your baby. Who knew your story. Who called you sister.

The most unsettling part isn't seeing danger approach. It's turning around to find it was always there. Sitting at your table. Drinking your wine. Cataloging your vulnerabilities for future reference.

When Friends Aren't

The breastfeeding incident. That's what I call it now, though "incident" feels too small for what was essentially the friendship equivalent of a controlled demolition. Honestly, it should've been the end right then and there, the moment she revealed who she really was beneath all that performative sisterhood.

We were at Monster Jam, yes, the monster truck rally where grown men scream at vehicles named Grave Digger while drinking beer from plastic cups. My toddler sought comfort. The kind of comfort only I could provide. So, I breastfed him. Simple as that. Natural as breathing. The thing human bodies have been designed to do since the dawn of time, long before anyone decided breasts were primarily decorative.

But apparently, evolution hadn't consulted her personal comfort levels.

At an event where the main entertainment was watching trucks with names like "Bone Crusher" leap through the air while crowds cheer for automotive carnage, she found *my* breasts objectionable.

Let that sink in for a moment. (At least the trucks were upfront about their destructive intentions.)

I didn't notice it at the time, too focused on my child to catalog the facial expressions of women old enough to mind their own business. But my husband did. KB is my early warning system for social landmines, the canary in the coal mine of other people's bullshit.

When she caught sight of me nursing, she rolled her eyes. Not the subtle, accidentally-caught-myself kind of eye roll. This was theatrical. Deliberate. The kind of eye roll that requires core engagement and a complete abandonment of basic human decency. Like she needed to broadcast her discomfort to anyone within visual range, as if my child's need for nourishment was somehow a personal affront to her delicate sensibilities. (Because nothing says "supportive friend" quite like publicly shaming someone for feeding their baby).

The judgment was palpable. Her glance said everything she didn't, and none of it was kind. It was all there, even if I missed it in the moment.

The next day, she made it explicit. She suggested I wean him because she was uncomfortable with my public breastfeeding, as if my parenting decisions were hers to weigh in on.

The real offense wasn't what I was doing. It was that I wasn't embarrassed to do it.

I explained, politely, that I wasn't going to stop breastfeeding my child to appease someone else's discomfort. That my choices as a mother didn't require her approval or permission.

I reminded her that this wasn't just about nursing. That after everything I went through to even have a child...the cancer, the infertility, the miscarriages...I was asking for support.

What I got? A complete absence of compassion.

She hit me with "My feelings aren't attached to your story."

Which, if you think about it, is a bold way to say, *I hear you, I just don't care.*

That's when I finally understood what I'd seen in her eyes at Monster Jam. What chilled me wasn't just judgment about breastfeeding. It was something darker. Resentment.

As if my survival offended her.

As if she would've preferred I hadn't made it through cancer, through infertility, to me feeding my son.

Like it would've been easier for her if my body had failed. If I failed.

Not just her discomfort. But the sense that she looked at me and wished I hadn't lived.

I thought about it. I thought about how much I suddenly didn't like her. So, while she was busy untangling her feelings from my story, I was busy untangling her from my life.

Her discomfort wasn't subtle. It wasn't accidental. It was performative, deliberate. The kind of eye roll that says, "Everyone look at how tolerant I'm being."

She didn't need to comment, but she did.
She didn't need to center herself, but she did.

Women like her think closeness gives them the right to comment. They mistake proximity for permission.

Why would I care about the unsolicited opinions of a frumpy, middle-aged woman who had clearly never met a boundary she couldn't bulldoze?
Her discomfort was her problem. Not mine.

Weeks later, I brought it up again. I thought maybe she'd want to repair the damage. Maybe she'd understand how her reaction made me feel dismissed. Unseen. Disrespected.

I thought maybe she'd apologize. Or at least pretend to care.

Instead, she doubled down. "How did you think I would feel? Seeing you breastfeed a toddler..."

Bitch, I didn't. Why would I think about *you* while comforting my child?

The fracture was instant.
One moment, connection.
The next...absence.

Silence where friendship once lived. Like coming home to find all your furniture gone. The walls still standing, but the warmth vanished. No note.

Just rooms echoing with the ghost of laughter.

That was the moment I realized it wasn't about breastfeeding, or even about me. It was about her. Her discomfort, her judgment, her inability to see beyond herself. She had taken something deeply personal, a moment between me and my child, and made it about herself.

...

I met her in high school. Not college, not as adults finding our way. High school, when everything feels both temporary and eternal. When friendships are formed in the crucible of adolescent insecurity and shared survival. During that raw, unfinished time when you're still figuring out who you are, let alone who your friends should be.

For almost thirty years, she was a fixture in my life. She knew the girl I was before I became the woman I am. Through bad dates and devastating heartbreaks. Through midnight confessions and sunrise promises. Through the uncertain years of early adulthood when we were both trying to build lives that made sense. Birthdays. Graduations. My wedding. The early days with Grayson. A witness to all the moments, big and small, that shaped me.

We had the kind of friendship I thought was weatherproof. The kind you assume will last forever, not because it's perfect, but because it's survived so much already. All that history creates a language between two people, a shorthand I mistook for unconditional understanding.

But what looks like depth from above can still be shallow underneath. We didn't drift apart slowly, the way some friendships do. There was no gentle untethering, no slow erosion, no gradual realization that we'd become different people. One day, we were close. The next, her words sliced through decades of history, leaving a wound too deep to ignore.

"My feelings aren't attached to your story."

Seven words. Seven words that revealed everything.

It took her seconds to say them. It took me months to stop hearing them.

...

I should have seen it coming sophomore year.

We were at her house after school, sprawled across her bedroom floor doing homework. I was struggling with algebra (numbers have never been my friends) and she was breezing through calculus like it was a crossword puzzle.

"Ugh, this is impossible," I muttered, erasing the same equation for the fourth time.

"You're not a math person," she said without looking up from her textbook. "You're more...creative."

The pause was everything. That tiny hesitation where she chose her words carefully. Where she decided what version of support to offer.

The way she said "creative" wasn't a compliment. It was pity dressed up as encouragement. The kind of thing you say when you can't bring yourself to lie outright but don't want to tell the truth either. As if being creative was the consolation for not being smart enough for the things that actually mattered.

Even then, at sixteen, something in my chest tightened. Not because I believed her assessment of my intelligence, but because I recognized the pattern. The subtle superiority. The way she positioned herself as the generous one, offering crumbs of validation to someone clearly beneath her.

I should have paid attention to that feeling. Should have trusted the way my body recoiled from her charity.

Instead, I laughed it off. Told myself I was being sensitive. That she meant well.

Thirty years later, when she rolled her eyes at me feeding my child, I finally understood: she'd always seen me as less than. The math homework was just the first time she let it show.

The High Road Version

Friendships don't always last forever, and that's okay. I've outgrown people who aren't growing. People shift, stall, and sometimes just stay exactly where they are. I value the time we shared, and even though we are no longer in each other's lives, I wish her well.
From a distance.

Letting go of friendships can be bittersweet, but it also clears space for the relationships that actually feel like expansion, not maintenance.

If you'd prefer a more nuanced, emotionally mature reflection on this friendship, you may consider this your graceful exit. Skip ahead if you're not interested in the unfiltered truth.

But if you want the real story, the one without the smoothing, the softening, or the strategic omissions, keep reading.

I've buried enough truths for her comfort. This one gets to live.

...besides, you didn't come here for the high road.

The Low Road Version: Petty, Honest, and Unapologetic

That was the moment I realized she wasn't a real friend, not then, and maybe not ever. A real friend doesn't twist your choices into a personal attack or treat your family's needs like a public debate.

I was asking for empathy from someone who can't find it in the mirror. People who flinch at their own reflection don't have compassion to spare. It's hard to offer real support when you're too busy resenting anyone who stands firm in their choices.

Some people will hurt you and then act like you hurt them. They rewrite the story to make themselves the victim, and suddenly, you're the villain just for making a choice they couldn't control. (There's a special kind of gaslighting that happens when someone cuts you and then examines their own finger for paper cuts.)

When one friendship falls apart? Sometimes, it takes others down with it.

Later I heard that it wasn't just her. Another friend was upset because her husband saw me breastfeeding. As if I'd staged some kind of burlesque show in the middle of a café. Because god forbid breasts be used for anything besides decoration or male entertainment.

KB suggested I fuck all their husbands to even the score. But I'm not into revenge plots that end with me doing charity work.

One of them actually said, "People will have feelings about you breastfeeding in public." Of course they would. People have feelings about women existing. That wasn't my problem.

It wasn't quiet disagreement. It was coordinated silence. And that's louder than anything they could've said.

Apparently, when one friend in a group decides they don't like your choices, it becomes a team sport. A few weeks later, I noticed a distinct chill in the group chat. The kind where your messages are suddenly the last ones replied to, or not replied to at all. It was like watching a slow-motion edit of my life in real time, realizing I was the part being cut. (Edits always cut the best parts first.)

The final nail? I wrote about the experience on my blog, because that's what I do: I process by writing. Amazing how people can recognize themselves in a story where they're never actually named.

I simply...disappeared from their narrative. Erased with the ease of deleting a contact. The call had ended, the line gone dead. They hung up on me without even saying goodbye.

The silence after betrayal has a texture. Have you felt it? That thick emptiness where questions float unanswered. What did I miss? When did I become someone they could simply...unmake? Was I ever truly seen at all?

By the time Valentine's Day rolled around, I was down three friends. The irony wasn't lost on me. It stung.

But underneath the sting was something messier. Doubt that whispered in the dark: *What if you're wrong? What if you're overreacting? What if you just threw away thirty years over a misunderstanding?*

The doubt was almost worse than the betrayal. At least betrayal was clean. Doubt was quicksand.

...

The breastfeeding incident wasn't about breastfeeding. It was about respect. Anyone who can't honor your boundaries or support your choices doesn't deserve a seat at your table. When she refused to hear me, when she doubled down on her discomfort, I knew we weren't coming back from that. And in the end, she had the audacity to ask, "How can I know you won't write about me again?"

The nerve of it. The true betrayal wasn't in her judgment of my mothering, but in this naked attempt to control my voice. Yesterday's confidante becomes today's stranger in the space of a heartbeat. Solid ground transforms to thin ice beneath your feet.

No warning.
No creaking boards.

Just the sudden knowledge that the people who knew your stories were always taking notes. To rewrite you.

The thing about mistreating someone who writes: it's going to live on the page.
You don't get final cut.
You get documented.

You get immortalized.

If you wanted me to write warmly about you, you should've given me reason to.

But let's be honest, what she really meant was:
How dare you ruin my reputation by telling the truth about the things I said and did.

File this under dark comedy: she is a maternal mental health practitioner. Someone who should have understood the importance of support and choice in motherhood, but instead, chose judgment.
She gets paid to help women feel safe. She does the opposite for free.

The disconnect was as glaring as her eye roll. And in the end? Just as unforgivable.

I spent years beLIeviNg in her frienDShip, only to discover it was conditional on my silence...nearly three decades of history erased because I fed my child with my body instead of her approval. Seems her professional compassion expires the moment her personal discomfort begins.

Some chapters close quietly. Others slam shut.

...

Grief over friendships is a tricky thing. It doesn't follow any rules, and nobody brings you casseroles.

I find myself mourning the version of those friendships I thought I had. The ones where I could share my struggles, my values, my blog posts, and not worry about it all blowing up in my face. Those friendships weren't real. They were conditional. Conditional on me staying small, quiet, and agreeable. And, apparently, discreet about my boobs.

I'm proud of the boundaries I held. I wasn't going to stop breastfeeding in public to protect someone's delicate constitution. I wasn't going to muzzle myself just because the truth made someone squirm.

Let them be uncomfortable.
Discomfort's cheaper than self-betrayal.

For so long, I forgave the snide comments. The passive aggressive digs. I told myself they didn't mean it like that. I told myself a lot of things. (The lies we tell ourselves are always the most convincing ones.)

I didn't ignore that many little betrayals by accident. I ignored them because it felt safer than starting over. Even when I knew better. Maybe because I knew better.

It's easier to keep calling it friendship than admit it's something else entirely.

I wasn't ready to lose the history. Even when it stopped feeling like home.
History isn't always worth the weight it carries.

People who can't respect my choices don't deserve a front-row seat in my life.
Immortality comes for everyone who crosses a writer.

The real ones stayed.
The rest?

Maybe they should've weaned themselves off me sooner.

raising him, finding me

Nobody warns you about the way motherhood cracks you open.

Every feral instinct I'd ever buried suddenly surfaced, sharp and primal. The animal part of me that I'd been trying to make socially acceptable for thirty-nine years finally had permission to exist.

I remember staring at his sleeping face in those early days, my body hollow and aching, but strangely complete. Like I'd been walking around missing a limb I didn't know I had until he filled my arms. Not wondering if I'd survive this demolition, but marveling that I'd managed to exist before it.

The milk stains on every shirt. The constant, animal vigilance. The way my heart seemed to live outside my body now, suddenly vulnerable to absolutely everything.

Nobody talks about how terrifying it is to love someone this much.

One minute you're a person. The next, you're holding a stranger who feels like home, unsure if you'll ever sleep again, and somehow still convinced you were always meant to do this.

Everyone tells you to cherish it. To savor the newborn smell and the little noises and the miracle of it all. But no one warns you what it feels like when your identity dissolves. Not into nothingness, but into something unrecognizable.

No one tells you that your body becomes public property. That your time no longer belongs to you. That every choice you make will be dissected by strangers and relatives like it's a group project they never contributed to, but still feel entitled to grade.

I didn't feel lost in those early days. I felt certain. Not because it was easy, but because nothing had ever felt more right.

I looked at him, this tiny, intense, perfect human, and something shifted.

A hard reset. A click. A knowing.

There he was. Somehow, I knew him. Like my body had been waiting its whole life to hold this one person.

And in holding him, something in me stirred. Not a transformation exactly, more like a reckoning.

Motherhood forced me to confront the parts of myself I hadn't fully embraced. The parts that were "too much" for the world, but just right for my son.

...

The first time I held Grayson, after all those years of trying, after cancer and grief and loss, I felt a strange sense of recognition. Not just of him, this new person I somehow already knew. But of myself.

As if some essential part of me had been waiting for this moment to fully awaken.

The weight of him in my arms. The impossible softness of his skin. The way his entire hand wrapped around my finger, holding on with startling strength.

In that moment, I understood something I couldn't have before: becoming a mother wouldn't diminish me. It would ignite me.

Not less myself...
But more fierce.
More certain.
More alive.

More completely myself than I'd ever been.

I wish that clarity had insulated me. That becoming a mother, becoming *this* mother, meant the world would back off and let me be.

The first test came from family. It's always the ones who share your blood who feel entitled to drain it.

My uncle decided postpartum was the ideal window for literary collaboration. Apparently, it's prime ghostwriting season.

Never mind that I had a full-time job. Never mind that I was bleeding, leaking, and barely sleeping.

He couldn't grasp that I was busy building something far more demanding than editing his manuscript: a nervous system for a brand-new person.

It's ironic someone so obsessed with crafting his legacy couldn't recognize that I was busy living a story of my own.

His voice carried that familiar disappointed tone: "You always have time for that child, but never for family obligations."

That child. As if my son were a distraction instead of the main event.

In Iranian culture, family obligation isn't a request. It's a commandment. When an elder asks for help, you don't get to say no. You don't get to have other priorities. Your time, your energy, your life belongs to the family hierarchy first.

My uncle wasn't just asking for a favor; he was invoking generations of cultural expectation. The unspoken rule that family comes before everything, including your own child.

And I chose differently.

When I didn't comply, he told me not to spoil my son, as if spending time with him was indulgent. Which, to be fair, it is, in that scandalous way that only good parenting can be.

I guess in his world, parenting is only valid if it looks like neglect.

His version of parenting had more to do with optics than connection. His disappointment was loud, but my resolve was louder.

I thought of my own childhood. Of conversations that stopped when I entered the room, as though my presence were an interruption to the real business of being adults. Of my mother's sharp "STOP CRYING" whenever tears came, not because she cared why I was upset, but because my sadness disrupted her peace. How I learned children were meant to be seen and not heard, managed rather than known.

I spent decades making myself smaller in rooms like that. Then I had a son, and the math changed.

I promised myself he wouldn't be background noise. His tears wouldn't require silence. His feelings wouldn't need permission to exist.

"I'm sorry you feel that way," I told my uncle, not sorry at all. "But this is how I parent."

He didn't take it well. Still doesn't. Years later, he brings it up like I'm a defendant in a case he refuses to close.

Apparently, my no just meant he needed to rephrase the question.

...

Motherhood hasn't just changed my relationships with others...
It's transformed the one I have with myself. With my body. With my boundaries.

Before my son, I thought strength meant never breaking.
Now I know it means breaking, and then rebuilding, over and over again, without losing who you are underneath the rubble.

I used to wonder if I was too much.
Too opinionated. Too loud. Too demanding.
Now I understand that my too-muchness is exactly what my son needs: a mother who doesn't retreat into shadows to make others comfortable.

On difficult days, when exhaustion hums in my bones and doubt starts whispering, I look at him and think: *This is worth it. You are worth it.*

Even when the world whispers that I should be less.
Less loud. Less opinionated. Less protective.

I choose to be more.
More present.
More honest.
More feral in my love for him.

Because that's what he deserves. A mother who stands in her truth, even when it's inconvenient for others.

My body, once a battleground of shame and disappointment, became something sacred through loving him.
The body that survived cancer.
The breasts that fed him.
The arms that ached to hold a child now know the weight of being his safe place.
The heart that broke with loss now swells with every defiant little grin, every "mama," every reminder that this was never guaranteed.

This is the alchemy of motherhood.
Turning pain into power, scars into structure.

...

I didn't expect that in raising Grayson I would find my father again.

Not in some mystical way. In the fiercest, most practical way possible. In the moment I first said no to someone who expected me to fold. In the way I trusted my instincts over their opinions. In how I refused to apologize for taking up space.

The self my father saw and protected was suddenly protecting my son.

I catch glimpses of my father in Grayson's stubborn concentration. In the way he questions everything with those cataloging eyes that don't miss a thing. In how he laughs like the world just told him the best joke he's ever heard.

And I think: This is what my father would have loved most about him. The refusal to be anyone other than exactly who he is.

There are moments when I'm defending a boundary or standing my ground, and I can almost hear my father's voice: *That's my girl.* Like he's been waiting all these years for me to remember who I was before the world told me to be smaller.

My father didn't teach me how to be a mother. But he taught me how to be unbreakable.

When they question. When they condescend. When they dress it up as concern.
I think of him.
I think of the daughter he raised to trust herself above all else.

Because that's what he would have wanted for both of us. To take up all the space we were meant to fill.

...

The hardest lesson of motherhood has been learning to trust myself. To mute the chorus of unsolicited advice, polite disapproval, outdated opinions, and listen to the voice that actually knows what my son needs.

There are nights when he wakes and wants only me. When my presence is the comfort no article or expert could replace. Moments when our eyes meet across a room, and I know exactly what he's thinking without a word passing between us.

This is the language we're building together. The sacred text of our relationship that others can't read or interpret.

At three, someone got too close to him at the library and he calmly sang, *"get back, motherfucker. You don't know me like that."*
Effective boundary-setting starts early.

Good parenting isn't about raising polite children. It's about raising children who can drop Ludacris quotes in the perfect moment.

And one day in the car, I caught him singing, *"I've got hopes in different area codes."*
Ludacris would be proud. Or confused. Possibly both.
I couldn't stop laughing. What a beautiful misfire.
He took a song about objectification and made it aspirational. Turned it into hope. Accidental poetry.
He made it *his*.

I've learned that good parenting rarely looks impressive from the outside. It's not curated milestones or flawless public behavior. It's teaching your child that politeness isn't more important than self-preservation. It's apologizing when you get it wrong. It's creating safety in a world that feels increasingly unsafe.

And sometimes, it's walking away from anyone who can't respect the boundaries you've drawn around your family.

...

He doesn't need to be good to be loved. I'll make sure he knows that. Early and often. He doesn't have to chisel away parts of himself to fit into someone else's expectations. He just has to be him. Bold. Messy. Unapologetic.

I hope he learns that some losses are worth it. That comfort isn't always the prize, it's often the trap. That the right people will stand beside him, even if no one else does.

I watch him now. Fierce. Certain. Unbothered. Unaware that the world will try to tame him. And I make a promise he'll never hear: *I won't be the first one to make you doubt yourself.*

When he tells me "my heart is full of you," I know what matters. Not the judgments, or the expectations, or the traditions. Just this. Just us. Just this connection that transcends explanation.

My hope isn't that he'll be perfect. It's that one day, when he's sitting in therapy, it's not because I chose someone else's ego over his childhood. *(It's because I've given him just enough damage to be interesting at parties.)*

...

Some days, motherhood feels like drowning in shallow water. Like you can stand, but it still steals your breath.

And then he'll do something stubborn. Or brilliant. Or infuriatingly familiar. And I'll see myself in him. Chaotic. Creative. Too much.

That's the thread. Not just to him, but to everyone who made me.
My father, who taught me to question everything.
My mother, who did what was expected while quietly resenting it.
The women in my lineage who did what they had to with what they had.
And me...who didn't survive just to disappear.

I'm not raising him with martyrdom. I'm raising him with fire.

Being worse at playing the role. Worse at seeking approval. Worse at molding myself into what they wanted.
That made me better at the things that actually matter.
Better at loving him exactly as he is.
Better at showing him what self-respect looks like.
Better at building something honest.
Where we don't pretend.
Where the truth isn't punished, even when it's inconvenient.

Not to be good by someone else's standards, but to be true by our own.

I'm not raising him to be easy. I'm raising him to question everything. Even me.
Because being "good" is usually just code for being convenient.
For staying quiet when you should be raising hell.

The world calls it "worse" when a mother refuses to disappear.

When she maintains her voice, her boundaries, her distinct self.
When she isn't willing to be erased by her own devotion.

And if that makes me worse, I'll take it.
Not just for me, but for him.
Let him witness a mother who chose herself.

They call it worse when a mother stays whole.
When she lets her child see it all.
Ambition. Flaws. Rage. Love. Unedited.
The blueprint for what I'm supposed to be: Soft-spoken. Tireless. Sacrificial.

The looks I get when I'm out with Grayson are priceless.
The shock when I don't rush to solve his every problem.
The judgment when I talk to him like a person instead of cooing in baby talk.
The horror when I admit that my life still belongs to me, too.

"But you're a mother now," they say, as if reproduction should have lobotomized me.

Yes, motherhood transformed me. I became obsessed with Grayson in a primal, almost frightening way I could never have anticipated. I'd lift a car off that kid. I'd fight a bear.
That love? It's feral. It's oxygen. It terrifies me in the best way.
But it didn't erase me. It didn't replace my personality with some generic maternal software update.

I'm still me. The loud, opinionated, ambitious me.
Just me, with a child I'd die for. Without hesitation.

As if giving birth should have erased every non-maternal thought from my brain.
Can you imagine how boring this book would be if it had?

I'd rather Grayson see a whole human than a sanitized, self-sacrificing caricature.
I'd rather he know me in all my complicated, ambitious, sometimes selfish glory than offer him an airbrushed version of maternal perfection.

If that makes me worse, fine.
I've never trusted the people who confuse devotion with disappearance.
Even when motherhood became the loudest thing in me, I didn't mute the rest.

the art of disappointing people

Most people spend their whole lives avoiding disappointing others. I turned it into an art form.

Technique. Timing. Precision I only got with practice. I learned to read expectations the way some people read sheet music. Then decided exactly which notes to leave out.

Every disappointment was a choice: betray them or betray myself.

The first person I disappointed was my mother. (The last one too, when she reads this.)

I must have been five or six.
I did something time-out worthy. No idea what.
What I remember: her stern voice. Her finger pointing at the corner.

"Think about what you've done."
I nodded solemnly. Trudged to my designated punishment spot.

When she found me, curled up and peaceful instead of remorseful, her exasperation was immediate.
This wasn't how time-outs were supposed to work. I was supposed to feel bad. Absorb the lesson. Emerge transformed.
Reflect. Apologize. Instead, I took a nap.

Even then, I knew how to disappoint people by refusing to perform as expected.

...

In second grade, my teacher asked us to write about what we wanted to be when we grew up. While other kids scribbled astronauts and veterinarians, I wrote: "I want to be left alone."

Mrs. Peterson's face when she read it was a masterpiece. She sent a note home to my parents expressing "concerns about my attitude." My father framed it. Told people I was a visionary.

...

There's a particular ache that comes with watching someone's face fall when you don't meet their expectations.
A tightness in your chest. A split-second doubt.
Maybe I should have just gone along with it?

I collected disappointments like souvenirs from countries I'd never wanted to visit.
Passport stamps from guilt trips.
Return tickets to "I thought you'd be nicer."

The boyfriend who wanted a girlfriend who didn't "make everything an issue."
The boss who wished I would "just take direction" without questioning the strategy.
The friend who needed me to stay small so she could feel big.
The relative who thought a good daughter would've chosen differently.

I spent years trying to contort myself into shapes that would fit their expectations.
Holding my tongue. Dimming my fire. Swallowing words that burned.

Until I realized: their disappointment wasn't my failure. It was my freedom.

...

Some disappointments free you. Others leave an empty space where someone used to be.

I had a friend. A real one. The kind earned through late-night conversations and shared emergencies. Someone who knew my stories before they became chapters. And then I didn't.

It's unsettling to watch a friendship disappear not because it changed, but because someone else couldn't handle it existing.

His girlfriend's insecurity wasn't my problem, except that suddenly, it was. With a single conversation (one I wasn't even part of), I lost a friend. Not from distance or damage, but because someone else's fragility outweighed our connection.

What bothered me most wasn't his absence. It was the erasure. Years of platonic friendship rewritten as something suspicious because someone couldn't imagine that a man and woman could share thoughts, jokes, naked photos, and support without it meaning something.

(Apparently, my very existence threatens relationships.)

I wanted to be angry at him. For caving. For choosing peace over authenticity. For letting someone else dictate the geography of his life.

But I understood the calculus. The daily comfort versus the occasional friendship. The path of least resistance.

Still, I couldn't help but think: What kind of love demands you amputate parts of your life? What kind of partnership is built on restriction rather than expansion?

The loss clarified my boundaries. I won't police anyone's heart to feel secure. I'd rather be alone than build walls around someone I love.

And maybe that's the real loss. Not my friendship, but his chance to experience love without conditions. Without surveillance. Without insecurity disguised as concern.

...

Not everyone sees me as a threat. Some people just see me.

KB found me late one night, staring at my phone.
I'd been nodding and smiling in a group text for hours, agreeing to plans I had no interest in, laughing at jokes that weren't funny.

I'd just enthusiastically agreed to dinner at a restaurant where the chef seemed to hate people and cooking.

Playing the agreeable, easy-going friend who never makes waves.

"What are you doing?" he asked.

"Being likable," I said.

He looked at me.
"I didn't fall in love with likable," he said.
"I fell in love with you."

It was the permission I didn't know I'd been waiting for. Permission to be difficult. Demanding. Disappointing. Myself.

...

The next day, my friend group was planning another beige social gathering. The kind where everyone drinks just enough to pretend they're having fun, but not enough to say anything real.

The restaurant they chose was overpriced, underwhelming, and specialized in small portions no one enjoyed eating.

When they asked for my thoughts, I broke script.

"I'd rather chew glass than go back to that restaurant," I typed. "The food tastes like it was prepared by someone who hates both cooking and humans. Last time, I stopped for a burger on the way home."

The group chat fell silent.

Three typing indicators appeared, disappeared, reappeared.

Finally, someone replied, "Where would you prefer to go?"

Such a simple question. Revolutionary.

I suggested a dive bar with incredible street tacos. Music too loud for small talk. Food too messy for pretension.

They agreed.

That night was different. More laughter. Actual conversation. Someone confessed they were thinking of quitting their job. Another admitted their marriage was struggling. Real humans emerged from behind their social personas.

Being unlikable opened the door to being known.

…

The art of disappointing people isn't about malice.

It's not about taking pleasure in letting others down.

It's knowing that carrying their expectations usually means dropping your own.

It's about knowing when to say:
I can't make it to that dinner.
I don't agree with that opinion.
I hate your boyfriend.
Your shirt is hideous.
I won't apologize for taking up space.
I'm not responsible for your feelings.
I won't apologize for breastfeeding in public just because you're jealous.
No.

No is the shortest sentence I've ever been punished for saying. Sometimes the punishment comes from saying what everyone else wants left unsaid.

...

We were at dinner with friends when someone said everything happens for a reason.

I'd been sitting with loss for years. Not the cinematic kind that ends with catharsis, but the quiet, ongoing kind. The kind people try to neaten with platitudes.

I'd heard "everything happens for a reason" after my father died. After my diagnosis. After moments that never had a reason.

Hearing it again wasn't just tone-deaf. It was erasure. It reduced the rawness of my lived experience into something spiritual and digestible. Made my grief a lesson plan instead of something I actually had to survive.

I said it doesn't.

They smiled like I was being difficult. Like I didn't understand the assignment of comfort.

"Some things just happen," I said. "And then you have to live with them. There's no reason. No lesson. Just the living with it."

Silence. The clink of a glass. Someone topped off their wine like they could drown the discomfort.

Someone changed the subject to vacation plans.

The air had shifted. You could feel it. The subtle distancing that happens when you stop being easy to digest.

Later, a friend texted: *You okay? You seemed...heavy tonight.*

It wasn't concern. It was discomfort dressed up as care.

I didn't explain myself. I'd already done that for years. Translating grief. Softening truth. Making my pain digestible for people who couldn't sit with it.

This time, I let their discomfort stand.

I wasn't trying to shock anyone. I was just tired of being fluent in euphemism.

Approval is easy to earn when you have none of your own. Self-respect costs more. Most people can't afford it.

...

Being unlikable in service of someone you love feels like justice. Being unlikable to terrible people feels like art.

But the hardest disappointments? Those happen at home.

Motherhood is a masterclass in disappointment. Mutual. Relentless. Weirdly intimate.

I disappoint Grayson constantly. I say no to ice cream before dinner, to staying up late, to narrating a detailed monologue while I'm on a call.

He looks at me like I've just cancelled childhood itself. His face crumples. His lower lip trembles. He calls me "the meanest mom EVER" with the conviction of a boy who has known great suffering. (And he has. For months, the store was out of the strawberry goat cheese he loves.)

And he disappoints me too. He forgets to say thank you. Leaves his toys out after I've asked him three times to clean them up. Shrugs off my hug when I've been thinking about holding him all afternoon.

But here's what we're learning together:
We can let each other down and still be okay.

Still be safe.
Still be us.

Nothing explodes.
The world keeps spinning.

The love stays.

Connection doesn't disappear just because someone doesn't give you what you want. Disappointment doesn't mean disconnection. Love doesn't always say yes. But it always shows up.

...

I've disappointed men who wanted me to be smaller, quieter, less demanding (it's been a pleasure, truly).

I've disappointed friends who expected me to hand out pieces of myself like party favors.

I've disappointed family members who believed tradition should trump personal happiness.

I've disappointed plenty of people who think likability is a moral obligation.

I've disappointed myself when I've fallen short of my own expectations.

But with each disappointment, I've grown more comfortable in my own skin.
More certain of my worth.
More willing to name what I need.
Less interested in managing how it lands.

...

I wasn't built for people-pleasing, but I tried it when the pressure felt too heavy to ignore.

I think of the moments I spent anticipating what others wanted. Chasing expectations I never agreed to. Saying yes when every cell in my body was screaming no.

Being "worse" at people-pleasing has made me better at everything else.

Better at my work, because I no longer dilute my expertise to make men comfortable. Better at friendship, because the ones who are still here want the real me. Better at motherhood, because my son sees you can have boundaries and still be loved.

Better at living, because I stopped trying to earn the right to exist.

...

People like to cast me as the villain. I relate to villains in stories. Their refusal to conform. Their willingness to be disliked for standing their ground. I have a deep-rooted respect for women who get mad in public and don't flinch when they're called bitchy.

I am the kind of worse that disappoints with precision. That doesn't pad a no with explanation or apology. That doesn't soften refusals with maybes or somedays.

I am worse at meeting expectations that require me to abandon myself. Worse at maintaining relationships where I'm valued for what I provide instead of who I am. Worse at keeping the peace when peace is just another word for surrender.

The kind of worse that maintains eye contact while someone's insulting me, and smiles because it's about to be my turn.

I don't just disappoint people. I confront them with possibilities they never allowed themselves. The ones who hate me for it remain imprisoned. The ones who thank me later have found their own kind of worse.

Each disappointment was a brick in the foundation of my life. Each no was a yes to myself.

···

There are people you'll choose not to disappoint. Your children, when they need your protection. Your partner, when they need your honesty. Yourself, when you're standing at the crossroads of integrity and convenience.

I choose carefully. I disappoint generously. The people worth keeping will love you not despite your boundaries, but because of them.

Not for how well you meet their expectations.
For how boldly you honor your own.

That's the art of disappointing people.
Not as a weapon.
As survival.
Not as failure.
As self-respect.

Self-preservation isn't selfish.
Every time I've swallowed my needs to please someone else, I've paid for it later.
In sleepless nights.
In resentment that bled into other relationships.
In the slow erosion of my own reflection.
I would rather disappoint everyone else than wake up one day and not recognize myself.

Being worse at pleasing others has made me better at knowing which bridges to burn.

Because disappointment isn't the end.
It's the beginning.
Sometimes it's the match that lights the flame.

burning bridges, building wings

I keep a running list on my phone. Not groceries. Not tasks. Names of people I no longer speak to. Thirty-seven entries and counting.

Thirty-seven people who once had access to me. Who I loved, trusted, gave pieces of myself to. Who taught me that disappearing isn't cruel. It's curated.

The list started accidentally. One deleted contact became two. Two became a habit. Now it's a ritual.

I see clearly when something stops working. When words no longer match actions. When promises fade into excuses. When respect erodes. When people trade truth for peace.

Others might linger in that gray space. Might normalize the slow dimming of their light.

Not me.

I recognize when something breaks beyond repair. When cracks become canyons. When staying costs more than setting fire to the exit.

Then one day, something shifts.

It isn't dramatic. No screaming matches. No ultimatums. Just a quiet moment when I finally admit the truth.

This isn't working.
This isn't right.
This isn't enough.

Then I burn it all down.

I've never met a bridge I didn't want to burn.

...

My mother says I inherited my father's stubbornness. She makes it sound like a birth defect.

Maybe it is. I inherited his stubbornness like other people inherit their grandmother's fine china. Something valuable, even if no one knows what to do with it.

Or maybe I finally understand what she never did: sometimes burning bridges isn't destructive.

Sometimes it's the only way to build your wings.

...

The first bridge I burned was my first boyfriend.

Three years of my teenage heart, gone in a fifteen-minute conversation. I still remember his face, how disbelief gave way to anger, then to that awful pleading look. As if he might find the right words. As if the right words would've changed my mind.

But there were no right words. There hadn't been for months.

I'd rehearsed what to say. How to soften the blow.
But in the moment, all the careful phrases evaporated, leaving only the raw truth:
I don't love you anymore.
Maybe I never did.
Cruel, yes. But kinder than pretending.

He started to cry. Then, in what felt like slow motion, he picked up an army boot and began hitting himself in the head with it.

An army boot.

Reader, I wish I were making this up.

I didn't know whether to grab his arm or leave.

The absurdity made it feel unreal, like I was watching it happen to someone else.

I walked away feeling like a monster.
And I wish I could say that wasn't true.

The weight of expectation lifted with each step.

Guilt and relief tangled in my chest, neither one winning.
Both true.

I walked for hours that night. No destination. Just motion. My phone buzzed until I killed it.

What kind of person leaves like that? I wondered. What kind of person feels relief in someone else's pain?

It took years to understand:
The monster wasn't me.

It was the belief that my happiness should come second to someone else's comfort. That I should swallow the truth just to spare someone else's pain.

...

I burn bridges with intention. Why would I take the high road when the low road has better stories?

I don't do it in anger. Anger leaves room for regret, for second thoughts, for the desperate midnight call that undoes all my resolve.

I do it in clarity. In the quiet certainty that comes after you've exhausted every other option.

I do it with kindness. Where possible. With honesty always.

And then, this is the crucial part. I don't look back.

Not because I don't care.

But because I finally care enough about myself to keep walking.

Not all bridges burn the same way. Some go up in a flash. Others smolder for years before I realize the structure's already gone.

The fire that changed everything started the day my father died.

...

The day my father died, my phone rang as his body was still warm. His scent lingered in the room. Sterile and hollow. Like something important had already left. My boss's name flashed on the screen.

"I heard about your dad," she said without a pause for condolence. "What's your plan for returning to work?"

My plan? My PLAN? The universe had just collapsed into a black hole, and this corporate vulture wanted to know when I'd be back to editing documents.

I had spent weeks by his bedside watching cancer hollow him out cell by cell. Watching the strongest man I knew become someone who needed help to sip water through a straw. And now he was gone, and my boss couldn't wait a single day before asking when I'd be back at my desk.

I don't remember what I said. Something polite. Something vague. Something that betrayed none of the white-hot rage building in my chest. I was still operating on autopilot, moving through the motions of being "professional."

But something hardened in that moment. Some fundamental understanding calcified in my bones. I wasn't asking for corporate loyalty. I was asking for basic human decency. The bare minimum of compassion that should exist between people who spend forty hours a week together.

Two weeks later, while I was still on bereavement leave, my phone rang again. "We need you to come in for a meeting," my manager said. "Just to discuss your transition back."

Transition back? As if grief was a temporary assignment I'd completed.

I walked into the building expecting to return to my office, my projects, my life. Instead, they escorted me to a conference room I'd never seen before.

"We've made some organizational changes while you were out," my manager said, not meeting my eyes. "We think a fresh start might be good for you."

"What kind of fresh start?"

"A different role. Different department. Less pressure."

Less pressure. Less visibility. Less everything.

"You're demoting me."

"We're offering you an opportunity to ease back into—"

"You're demoting me because my father died."

The silence was deafening.

They'd already packed up my office. Years of work, boxed up like evidence of a crime. My nameplate removed. My projects reassigned.

I never got to say goodbye to that version of my professional life. They killed it while I was burying my father.

Corporate America doesn't just lack compassion. It punishes you for needing it.

That's when I knew. It wasn't just my boss. It was the entire system. A machine designed to consume your time while giving nothing back. A culture that saw my humanity as an inconvenience rather than a reality.

They called it restructuring. I called it what it was: retaliation.

I stayed long enough to secure another job, then quit with zero remorse. No tearful goodbyes. Just brutal honesty in my exit interview about why I was leaving.

Society pretends there's nobility in swallowing your dignity for a paycheck. In showing up and smiling while your wounds are still raw. They call it professionalism. Dedication. Work ethic.

I call it capitalism's greatest con. The belief that your value is tied to your productivity, even when your world is crumbling. The expectation that you'll prioritize client deliverables over processing pain.

That wasn't the last time work betrayed me. It was just the first time I was too wrecked by grief to fight back.

Years later, at a different job, it wasn't one big betrayal. It was a slow grind of small corruptions: ethical lines blurred, corners cut, and the label of "difficult" reserved for anyone who didn't smile and comply.

Eventually, it didn't matter how ethical I was. The culture had already decided I was the problem.

So I became one.

...

Some bridges aren't just burned. They're detonated.

Some relationships leave no choice. The words still echo in my head sometimes. The way my cousin weaponized my infertility, her voice cold and deliberate: "The reason you can't get pregnant is because you'd be a bad mom."

Words like knives, aimed at the softest part of me. My greatest fear spoken aloud by someone who was supposed to love me. Family. Blood. The person who should have been a shelter became the storm.

It wasn't random cruelty. It was calculated. She knew exactly where I was most vulnerable and chose to strike there. All because I had set a boundary. Because I dared to have a relationship with her sister, to exist in the complicated space between their conflict. As if my loyalty could only be measured in complete allegiance or total abandonment.

In that moment, something crystallized inside me. Some words can't be taken back with a casual "sorry" months later. Some bridges aren't worth rebuilding.

Cruelty speaks more about the person wielding it than the person receiving it. Her words were a reflection of her own brokenness. Her inability to see beyond her narrow world. To understand that family isn't about control. It's about connection.

She collected wounds like trophies. Always keeping score. Always looking for the soft spot. The place where her words would hurt the most.

Some wounds don't need forgiveness to heal. They just need distance.

Sometimes the bridges you burn light the way to better ones.

...

The friends who fell away after I had Grayson taught me something important about bridges: some collapse under their own weight, without any help from you.

The unanswered texts. The cancelled plans. The growing silence where inside jokes used to live.

I mourned them at first, those friendships that couldn't survive the shift in my priorities. The women who wanted the old me, the one who could meet for spontaneous happy hours and weekend getaways.

The one who didn't have a tiny human dependent on her body, her presence, her constant attention.

But absence teaches too.

It showed me which connections were circumstantial and which were soul-deep. Which friends could love the mother as well as they'd loved the maiden. Which ones made space for all my evolving selves.

Those bridges, I reinforced. I tended them with what little energy I had left at the end of long days. I carried Grayson across them, introducing him to the people who loved me enough to love him too.

The others...I let go.

Am I still angry about some of them? Yes.

A small flame that refuses to die. The whispered judgments. The subtle eye rolls. The ways my motherhood became inconvenient to friendships that once felt unbreakable.

But I've learned that anger can illuminate too. It shows you what matters, what's worth fighting for. What's worth burning.

Some people are chapters, not the whole story.

...

The hardest bridges to burn are the ones I built myself, the stories I told about who I am and what I deserve.

I'm the responsible one. I'm the one who can handle it. I'm fine with less.

These are the bridges that loop me back into the same patterns. The same fights, the same compromises, the same slow bleed I kept calling a life. They're solid because I've marched across them a thousand times, even when I swore I wouldn't.

Burning them feels like betrayal. Like I'm abandoning some essential part of myself.

But that's the trick: those bridges aren't me. They're just the detours I built when I didn't know there were better roads.

...

No one tells you there's grief in freedom. In walking away. Even when staying would destroy you.

I've cried over every bridge I've burned. I've interrogated myself in the dark hours of the night. I've wondered if I'm fundamentally broken, incapable of the compromises that keep other people connected.

But morning comes, and with it, the certainty that settling for less than I deserve isn't noble.

It's surrender.

...

I've burned every kind of bridge there is. Relationships. Jobs. Versions of myself. Bridges built to move me in only one direction, away from who I really am.

I've walked away from people who couldn't love me completely. From opportunities that required me to diminish. From patterns that kept me small and safe and miserable.

And every time, in the light of those flames, I've discovered something:

Wings.

Not perfect ones. Not steady ones, at first.

But strong enough to carry me somewhere new. Somewhere true. Somewhere mine.

The gift of burning bridges isn't destruction. It's creation. The space to become something else. Someone else. Someone who doesn't need the old paths because she's learned to fly.

Is it selfish? Maybe.

Is it necessary? Absolutely.

I'm the kind of worse that terrifies people because I'm willing to lose everything rather than continue living on someone else's terms.

The kind that walks away from what most people would kill to have because I recognize the hidden costs. The kind that chooses uncertainty over guaranteed misery.

The kind that makes people uncomfortable because I'm a living reminder that they could leave too. Their dead-end job. Their soul-crushing relationship. Their suffocating social circle. If they were willing to be as "unreasonable" as I am.

But the world has a vested interest in your compliance. In your willingness to endure. In your fear of being labeled difficult, ungrateful, or too demanding.

Be agreeable, they say. Don't rock the boat. Think of everyone else first.

I'd rather choose freedom over belonging. I'd rather burn the bridge than keep crossing it with pieces of myself left behind each time.

You can stay on a bridge forever, suspended between what was and what could be.

Or you can set it aflame and trust that the fall will teach you everything you need to know about flying.

I choose the flames. Every time.

making sense
of the wreckage

I have a gift for making sense of chaos. Mostly because I'm usually the one who caused it.

But wreckage isn't random. It follows patterns. Leaves clues. And if you're paying attention, really paying attention, the debris tells a story.

My story is written in the things I destroyed. The bridges I burned. The relationships I walked away from. The versions of myself I left bleeding on the side of the road. Some of them deserved to die there.

Each piece of wreckage was a choice. Each scar, a lesson. Each ending, a beginning I didn't see coming. This isn't about learning from mistakes. This is about recognizing the difference between what I broke accidentally and what I broke on purpose.

And here's what I learned: my body always knew which was which.

...

My body knew the truth long before my mind was willing to acknowledge it.

The knot in my stomach when a friend said something that didn't align with her actions.

The tension in my shoulders during meetings with a particular colleague.

The subtle closing of my throat when a doctor dismissed my concerns.

These weren't coincidences or overreactions. They were warnings. My body recognizing danger before my mind could name it.

The first time I ignored those warnings, I was twenty-two and engaged to a man I didn't love. He was aggressively ordinary. Forgettable in every way except his desperation to be remembered. The world's biggest people-pleaser. (Who never pleased me.) The kind of man my mother would still call "a good catch." Mostly because he wore a collared shirt and had no visible tattoos.

But my body knew.

My chest tightened every time we talked about wedding venues.
Headaches appeared whenever we spent more than a day together.

Panic attacks ambushed me out of nowhere.
I felt relief when he worked late.

He wasn't even attractive.
I was out of his league then. Still am.

He just tried hard. Too hard.
Always performing.
Relentlessly agreeable.

He said what he thought people wanted to hear and
then wondered why no one really knew him.
Including me.

He proposed after two months. In public, of course.
Big crowd.
Lots of clapping.

The kind of moment designed for optics, not intimacy.

I didn't say yes. I didn't say no. I just stood there, smiling
like a hostage with a gun to her head made of social
expectations. Turns out love can't be negotiated.

Then I flew home and broke up with my actual
boyfriend. I figured if I was going to lie to someone, I
should at least narrow it down to one person at a time.

After that delightful conversation, I told myself I was
just nervous. That cold feet were normal.
That marrying someone who irritated me on a cellular
level was a perfectly reasonable next step.

He was desperate for validation.
He'd bend himself into a pretzel to avoid disappointing
anyone.

Every room was a new stage.
Every opinion, a threat.
My confidence made him insecure.
He treated nudity like it was against his religion.
The kind of man who probably apologized to mirrors.
I never once saw him naked.
I've gotten more intimate glimpses of strangers in
department store fitting rooms.

My directness made him defensive.
Anything that wasn't praise got filed under "personal
attack."
It was easier to say nothing than risk setting him off.
So I learned to hold my tongue. It was exhausting,
tiptoeing around someone who needed applause just to
feel okay.
He thought kindness was the same thing as likability. It
isn't.
He thought people-pleasing would make him lovable. It
didn't.
It just made him unknowable.

And if there's anything worse than being with someone
you don't love, it's being with someone who doesn't
even exist when the audience goes home.

I ignored all of it for months.
Until I couldn't anymore.

My dad's kitchen table.
Sunlight casting geometric patterns through the blinds.
The slight stickiness where someone had spilled orange
juice and wiped it up imperfectly.

The words tumbled out before I could second-guess them.
"I don't want to get married."

Relief hit like oxygen. Sudden. Undeniable. Necessary.

I expected questions. Concerns. Reminders about commitment and family expectations.
Instead, my dad nodded. Like he'd been waiting for me to see what he already knew.
"Then don't," he said simply.

I destroyed that engagement. I destroyed the version of myself that would rather perform love than live alone.

I didn't just call off a wedding. I walked away from a life I was supposed to want.
It didn't feel like loss. It felt like alignment.
Like finally saying no to a question I never meant to answer in the first place.

My mother was disappointed until she rewrote history. Now she says she always knew he wasn't right for me. She tells the story like she helped me pack.

His mother acted like I'd set their house on fire and pissed on the ashes. She questioned my character, my stability, my worth.
She'd already been making my life hell, policing my visits home, telling me I shouldn't see my family so frequently, warning him not to trust me because her husband had cheated on her. (To be fair, I had overlapped relationships getting into this one, but she didn't know that. And I was cheating on *him*...not her precious son.)

But really, she was mourning the fact that he'd never do better than me.
And time has proven her right.

I, on the other hand, absolutely did do better.

Last I heard, he's still chasing approval. Still trying to be everyone's favorite. Still exhausting.

Looking back, the signs were everywhere.
My body had been right.
It wasn't cold feet. It wasn't nerves.
It was self-preservation, dressed up as hesitation.

My body had already voted no.
Every forced smile. Every swallowed word.
Every time I lied and called it love.

First, it whispered.
Then, it screamed.

...

I used to call it anxiety. It wasn't. It was intuition with bad branding. I just didn't like what it was telling me.

For years, I second-guessed myself. Labeled gut feelings as overreactions. Brushed off internal warnings as paranoia.

That murmur? "This person isn't trustworthy."

That whisper? "This situation isn't right for you."

That internal scream? "Everything looks fine on paper but something is clearly off."

I called it overthinking. Or being too sensitive. Or complicating things that were supposed to be simple.

But it wasn't complication. It was clarity. My deepest wisdom trying to protect me from what my conscious mind wasn't ready to acknowledge.

My intuition didn't send formal invitations announcing its arrival. It showed up as "bad vibes" and "weird feelings" that I dismissed as overthinking. Meanwhile, anxiety was just running laps around worst-case scenarios, a hamster wheel of "what if" catastrophes.

They're not the same thing. One leaves you exhausted; the other saves your ass. That quiet voice telling me "something's off" knew the truth long before I was ready to admit I was walking straight toward a cliff.

I'd ignored that voice before in love, in friendship. Of course I ignored it at work too.

•••

Workplaces aren't built to nurture. They're built to extract. A truth written in my exhaustion.

For years, I poured myself into jobs.
Took pride in being the best.
The most thorough.
The most reliable.

I stayed late. Showed up early. Fixed mistakes I didn't make. Took on more work without more pay.

I thought my worth would be recognized. That excellence would be rewarded. That loyalty would be reciprocated.

Then came the cancer diagnosis.

I was thirty-five. Newly married. Facing surgery and an uncertain recovery. I needed support, understanding, time.

What I got instead was thinly veiled irritation. Inconvenient questions about project timelines. Subtle suggestions that perhaps this wasn't the right "fit" anymore.

They didn't say, "Your cancer is inconvenient for our bottom line."
They didn't have to.

It was in every pause. Every shift in tone. Every conversation where deadlines mattered more than my diagnosis.

The unspoken, but unmistakable message: Go die on your own time.

I was replaceable. A line item. A resource to be managed.

Corporate loyalty is an illusion. No job will love you back. Being exceptional didn't save me. It just made me easier to exploit.

I gave them everything. Time. Energy. Brilliance.
Even my good years.
Even the eggs I donated to capitalism by accident.

I loved my work.

It loved what it got from me.

I thought excellence meant salvation.
It only meant I was excellent at my own erasure.

I thought I was building a career. What I was really doing was constructing a cage. Brick by credential. Promotion by compromise.

The day I walked away wasn't a defeat. It was a liberation.

Being "worse" at work might have saved me. Less perfect. Less available. Less eager to please. I would've preserved my energy for what actually mattered. Modern workplaces hate two things: honesty and boundaries. The same two things that keep you sane.

The workplace that values your perfection over your humanity doesn't value you. It just knows how to sell you by the hour and replace you by the quarter.

I thought corporate indifference was cruel. Then, I discovered that some people who call themselves friends will abandon you just as quickly when you're vulnerable.

...

There was a miscarriage. Quiet. Unseen. Before KB. Before motherhood.

When I was still finding my footing in the world.

The physical pain was expected.

The emotional devastation was not.

The way it reopened childhood wounds, unresolved grief, questions about my worthiness and my body's capabilities.

No one sends flowers for losses that happen in silence. Just that same silence where sympathy should be. The particular loneliness of grieving something the world never knew existed.

I needed support. Turned to a friend. Someone I thought would understand. Someone who, years later, would decide public breastfeeding was my moral failing.

"It's because you took that medication," she said with cold certainty, naming something I hadn't actually taken. "That's what caused it."

As if my loss was a lesson. As if I had invited it through carelessness or ignorance.
She meant it as help. That's what made it violent.

I swallowed my hurt. Forgave the cruelty. Chalked it up to awkwardness around grief. The human tendency to invent causes when faced with the randomness of suffering.

Her later judgment of my mothering wasn't a betrayal. It was a continuation.

This wasn't about a miscarriage. Or my choices. This was about her fundamental discomfort with women's bodies functioning as nature intended. With the raw, primal reality of creation and nourishment.

Her first cruelty wasn't a fluke. It was information. A glimpse of something essential about how she viewed women. How she viewed me.

Forgiveness is a gift you give yourself, but it doesn't obligate you to keep people in your life.
Reconciliation without recognition isn't healing.
It's just pain rescheduled.

I forgave her then. I didn't later.
I bought myself a tennis bracelet instead.
At least it actually sparkles.

...

I used to fight everything.

Every snide comment. Every casual cruelty. Every willfully ignorant remark that someone dropped like a grenade and walked away from.

I appointed myself the corrector of wrongs. The educator of the unwilling. The voice in every room that wouldn't let bullshit slide by unnoticed.

As if my silence made me complicit. As if letting one terrible opinion pass meant I agreed with it.

The exhaustion nearly killed me.

Not the fighting itself (I love arguing). The constant vigilance. The way my nervous system stayed activated, scanning for the next battle. The energy drain of trying to teach people who had no interest in learning.

I was right. Almost always.

But being right was bleeding me dry.

Now? I pick my battles like I'm choosing which of my children to save. Ruthlessly. Strategically. With full knowledge that some things will burn while I protect what matters most.

Someone asks me if my hair is "natural" while reaching to touch it? I picture their hand in a blender.

Someone rolls their eyes at my kid for being a kid? They've just summoned the exact level of maternal fury that evolution designed for predator deterrence. I won't throw the first punch, but I'll memorize their license plate and their children's names.

My silence isn't agreement anymore. It's ammunition storage.

Saving my energy for wars worth winning.

···

The same clarity hit me about love.

If you're performing, it's not love. It's theater. Love dies the minute you start auditioning for it. Once you get the part, you're stuck playing a version of yourself you can't even stand.

I watched relationships around me. The compromises people made. The parts of themselves they silenced or hid to maintain peace. The endless negotiations of identity.

As if love were a contract with fine print no one had time to read.

I saw friends become shadows of themselves in relationships. Giving up interests. Changing opinions. Vanishing into someone else's idea of a partner.

The truth revealed itself slowly: real love doesn't require smoothed edges. The right people love because of complexity, not despite it.

Anyone who needs you to be less in order to love you more isn't offering love at all. They're offering control.

...

I keep learning the same lessons.

I spiral through the same patterns. Return to the same lessons at different levels. Face similar challenges with marginally less stupidity each time.

I still catch myself overextending sometimes. Still occasionally doubt my medical intuition when faced with dismissive professionals. Still feel that momentary sting when someone labels me difficult for having perfectly reasonable boundaries.

But I recognize these moments sooner now. Forgive myself more readily for the occasional backslide into old patterns.

Perfection isn't the goal. This becoming thing isn't about reaching some final, flawless state.

It's about remembering who I've always been beneath the layers of who I was taught to be.

Worse.

All that spiraling? All that tedious repetition?

I was supposed to break. All that loss, all that betrayal, all those moments when the ground gave way beneath my feet.

Instead, I came back sharper. Sharpened enough to cut.

What looked like wasted time wasn't wasted at all.

The relationships that didn't last. The jobs that didn't fulfill. The paths that led to dead ends.

None of it was a waste. They didn't break me. They forged me.

Every failure, every misstep, every blindside...it all serves now.

That friend's cruelty around my miscarriage taught me to recognize the pattern when it reappeared years later. Only then could I see it wasn't circumstantial, but fundamental to who she was.

Workplace betrayal taught me to recognize environments that operated like broken vending machines: insert effort, receive indifference.

Being dismissed by medical professionals taught me to trust my body's wisdom over external authority. To value my lived experience as expertise in its own right.

Every detour and disappointment left its mark. Every "wasted" moment was preparation for what would come next.

...

Everything I've learned, I've learned the hard way. Through mistakes. Through moments of clarity that arrived just in time to prevent me from repeating the same patterns, but too late to spare me the initial pain. The scars are syllabus now. Anyone trying to manage me should read them first.

And the most important thing I've learned? That I am the kind of worse that makes people uncomfortable because I refuse to pretend hard lessons make for neat stories.

The kind of worse that doesn't package pain into inspirational anecdotes. The kind of worse that acknowledges some wounds never fully heal, they just stop bleeding so obviously. The kind of worse that doesn't pretend suffering always has meaning.

The kind of worse that says sometimes life shatters you into pieces that will never fit back together the same way, and no amount of positive thinking will change that reality.

I'm getting worse at reassuring people that everything happens for a reason. Worse at finding silver linings when there aren't any. Worse at pretending trauma makes you stronger when sometimes it just makes you traumatized.

I'd rather be the kind of worse that tells uncomfortable truths than the kind of good that perpetuates comfortable lies.

i wish i was worse

I collect quotes like I collect grudges. Without shame. With the dedication of someone who knows it's probably unhealthy but enjoys it anyway. I've made peace with being petty.

Little fragments of recognition. Like someone reached inside my mind and yanked out a thought I hadn't named yet.

One of my favorites comes from Cher. Not from a song or a movie, but from an interview. Five words, delivered like she'd just solved a math problem: "I wish I was worse."

Five words that stopped me cold.

I wish I was worse.

Not better. Not more disciplined. Not more palatable. Not anything women are told to be.

Worse.

She didn't mean chaotic or cruel. She meant she wished she'd quit second-guessing herself sooner.

I recognized myself. All those years chasing "better" when "worse" was the answer.

Worse didn't mean reckless. It meant honest. Unapologetic. Feral. Unedited.

Cher didn't say it like a confession.
She said it like a regret sharpened into a revelation.
She could've gotten away with more, and she didn't.
That was her mistake.
(Her mistake, not mine. I've adjusted accordingly.)

That's when I started writing this book.

...

We're taught from birth that good is the goal.

Good girl.
Good daughter.
Good wife.

Each role its own leash. Short enough to keep you in line. Tight enough to leave a mark.

Each with its own impossible standard. Each with its own special method of erasure.

Be good.

Be better.
But what if worse is actually the answer?

What if worse just means honest?

...

I look at the women who came before me.

My grandmother. Softer. Quieter. More accepting of limitations. A woman who swallowed her dreams with her morning tea and called it contentment.

My mother. Wilder than her own mother, but still caught between freedom and obligation. She taught me what worse could look like even as she warned against it. The woman who told me to stay small while taking up space herself. A contradiction born not from hypocrisy, but from the divided heart of a woman caught between cultures, between her own freedom and her daughter's.

The expectations haven't changed. Only my willingness to meet them.

...

I think of all the versions of worse I've been.

The worse daughter who questioned authority.

The worse mother who refused to weave herself into a straitjacket of martyrdom.

The worse friend who set boundaries in a culture that calls them selfishness.

For every role, there was a script I was meant to follow. Words placed in my mouth by people who never asked what I wanted to say.

...

Being worse isn't easy.

There's a cost to authenticity in a world built on performance. A price for honesty in spaces designed for comfort. A consequence for boundaries in relationships accustomed to access.

I've lost jobs. Friendships. Opportunities. The approval of people whose love came with conditions I wasn't willing to meet.

I've been called difficult. Demanding. High maintenance. Too much. Not enough. A bitch. Unstable. Unprofessional. Unworthy. Stubborn. Selfish. Dramatic. Overwhelming. Uptight. Oversensitive. Hysterical. A problem. Bossy. Aggressive. Intimidating. Too loud. Too quiet. Too assertive. Not assertive enough. Prudish. Reckless. Calculating. Too emotional. Too logical. Heartless. Naive. Manipulative. Cold. Clingy. Needy. Distant. Unapproachable. Abrasive. Exhausting. A mess. A handful. Broken. Intense. Obsessive. Rude. Inappropriate. Shameless. Unreasonable. Ungrateful. Too independent. Too dependent. Impossible to please. Cruel. Bitter. Jaded. Rigid. Flaky. Unreliable. Hard to love.

All because I wanted the radical freedom of being myself.

...

But being worse? It's addictive. Once you stop performing, you can't go back to the theater.

It feels like waking up in your own skin after sleeping in someone else's for years.

Like finding your native language after speaking in translation your whole life.

Like breathing deeply after a lifetime of shallow sips of air.

...

I see it in other women too. The longing for worse.

I recognize the pattern. The careful shrinking. The reflexive apologies. The instinct to smooth every edge before speaking. Years of training in how to be palatable. How to stay just bright enough to be useful, but never blinding.

Sometimes I want to shake them. To say: *You're allowed to be certain. You're allowed to be right. You're allowed to take up space.*

But I understand. The world is kinder to women who play by the rules. Politeness keeps you employed. Deference keeps the peace. And invisibility? That's rewarded too, right up until you realize no one sees you anymore.

It's not a ladder. It's a trapdoor.

That's why their eyes light up when I say no without justification. The lean-in when I admit that I've chosen my needs over someone else's comfort.

Women are starving for permission to be worse. Permission I can't actually give them, but that I can model by refusing to package myself for approval.

...

Motherhood clarified it for me.

The first time someone told me I was spoiling Grayson by responding to his cries. The first time a stranger criticized my choices. When the pediatrician spoke to KB instead of me.

Something primal rose in me. Something that refused to be tamed or shamed or convinced that meeting my child's needs was somehow wrong.

If loving my son completely, responding to him consistently, trusting my instincts about his care makes me a worse mother by society's standards, then worse is exactly what I choose to be.

I've seen "better" mothering. The performance of it. The martyrdom of it. The slow erosion of self until there's nothing left but function.

I won't do it. I won't perform motherhood at the expense of being present for it. I won't sacrifice authenticity for someone else's approval.

I won't teach my son that love requires erasure.

...

What I want to give to Grayson isn't compliance training.

It's permission to be authentic, even when it's inconvenient for others.
The courage to disappoint the right people.
The audacity to choose truth over comfort.

Most of all, I want him to see what's possible when you refuse to meet expectations that were never designed for your happiness.

Authenticity doesn't guarantee everyone will like you.
It guarantees you'll like you.

...

My father knew this. Without having words for it, he understood.

"Don't let them dull your edges," he'd tell me when I'd come home crying about not fitting in. "The right people will love your sharp parts."

He was right. The people who belong in my life don't love me in spite of who I am.
They love me because of it.
Not in spite of my difficulty, but because I am difficult.
Not in spite of where I draw the line, but because I'm not afraid to draw it in permanent ink.

KB doesn't want me to be better. He wants me to be real.
Grayson doesn't need me to be perfect. He needs me to be present.

The right people want your worst. Your realest. Your most honest and unfiltered self.

...

I wish I'd been worse at convincing myself I had to handle everything alone.

The first time KB pumped my gas, I almost cried. Not because it was romantic. Not some grand gesture. Just that no one had done it since my dad.

Gas stations used to undo me.

KB didn't know any of that. He just got out of the car before I could and said, "I got it." No fanfare. No soundtrack. Just two people, one tank of gas, and the quiet relief of not having to do everything yourself.

Some forms of worse turn out to be exactly what you need. Worse at self-reliance. Worse at pretending you don't want someone to handle the small things.

I don't pump my own gas anymore. Somebody should get something out of this relationship.

...

I think of all the energy I wasted trying to be better.

The relationships I contorted myself to maintain.

The jobs I sacrificed my health for.

The boundaries I erased to avoid being labeled difficult.

All the times I chose to be good instead of real. To be better instead of honest. To be less instead of more.

Now imagine where that energy goes once you stop wasting it on restraint.

What it builds. What it burns.
What it leaves behind in its wake.
They'll whisper. They should. (I've given them so much material.)

...

Some days the old programming kicks in.
The default settings surface.
Say yes. Stay quiet. Make yourself smaller. Be nice.

Society spent decades installing that software.
Being worse feels fucking fantastic.
Every time I say no without explanation, something rewires.
Every time I tell the truth, even when it burns, I feel more solid.
Some days I'm gracious. Some days I'm uncompromising.
Some days I'm soft. Some days I bite.

That's the point. The trap wasn't just behavior. It was predictability.
And yeah, sometimes I still glitch. Still say yes when I should say no.

But I don't spiral about it anymore.
I don't grade myself on how authentic I was that day.

I just think: *Next time, I'll be worse.*

And that's not a promise. It's a threat.

That's exactly the kind of worse I want to be.
A menace.
The kind of worse that terrifies the status quo because it
proves the rules are unenforceable when we stop
enforcing them on ourselves.

...

Here's the truth beneath it all.

I didn't need to be better.
I needed to be worse.

Worse at obedience.
Worse at performing.
Worse at trading approval for belonging.
I didn't need to master silence.
I needed to master refusal.

Being worse isn't rebellion for the sake of spectacle.
It's reclamation.
It's about refusing to be erased.

It's time to be worse.

I've already begun.

the last word

They were right about me.
Just not in the way they thought.

I'm not the kind of worse that crashes and burns.
I'm the kind of worse that burns everything down and
doesn't look back.

My father knew this about me before I did.
"Don't let them dull your edges," he urged.
(As if I'd ever figured out how to be smooth.)

He's gone now, and I still hear his voice every time
someone tries to tell me I'm too much.
Too loud. Too honest. Too difficult.
Too whatever-word-they-use when they mean "stop
making us uncomfortable."

His death taught me that grief isn't something you can map out.
Neither is living.
People keep waiting for me to follow the rules.
I keep disappointing them.

Grayson arrived and rewrote everything I thought I knew about love.
Not because he completed me.
(What am I, a fucking jigsaw puzzle?)
But because he refused to be anything other than exactly himself.
Even when it was inconvenient.
Even when it was loud.
Even when it made other people nervous.

He gets that from me.

Nothing has reshaped me like loving him.
Nothing ever will.

KB fell in love with the worst parts of me.
The parts that argue with strangers.
The parts that say things that clear rooms.
The parts that refuse to pretend everything is fine when it isn't.
He fell in love with the real me.

I spent years trying to be likable.
Turns out, likable is exhausting.
Worse is liberating.

They warned me about what would happen if I stopped performing.
If I stopped shrinking.

If I stopped apologizing for taking up space.

They were right.
I became dangerous.
Not the kind that hurts people.
The kind that shows them what's possible.

Worse isn't what they told me it was.
It's what they were afraid I'd find inside myself.

Some people spend their whole lives trying to be good.
I spent mine trying to be real.
Real is messier.
Uncomfortable.
Unapologetic.

They were right to be afraid.
I'm not as dangerous as they suspected.

I'm worse.

I made peace with being the problem.
Villains get the best lines. And the last word.